OPPOSING
VIEWPOINTS®
SERIES

Education

Other Books of Related Interest:

"Congress shall make no law . . . abridging the freedom of speech, or of the press."

First Amendment to the US Constitution

The basic foundation of our democracy is the First Amendment guarantee of freedom of expression. The Opposing Viewpoints Series is dedicated to the concept of this basic freedom and the idea that it is more important to practice it than to enshrine it.

OPPOSING
VIEWPOINTS®
SERIES

Education

Noël Merino, Book Editor

GREENHAVEN PRESS
A part of Gale, Cengage Learning

GALE
CENGAGE Learning·

Detroit • New York • San Francisco • New Haven, Conn • Waterville, Maine • London

Elizabeth Des Chenes, *Director, Content Strategy*
Cynthia Sanner, *Publisher*
Douglas Dentino, *Manager, New Product*

© 2014 Greenhaven Press, a part of Gale, Cengage Learning.

WCN: 01-100-101

LIBRARY OF CONGRESS CATALOGING-IN-PUBLICATION DATA

Education / Noël Merino.
    pages cm. -- (Opposing viewpoints)
    Summary: "Opposing Viewpoints: Education: Opposing Viewpoints is the leading source for libraries and classrooms in need of current-issue materials. The viewpoints are selected from a wide range of highly respected sources and publications"-- Provided by publisher.
    Includes bibliographical references and index.
    ISBN 978-0-7377-6434-5 (hardback) -- ISBN 978-0-7377-6433-8 (paperback)
    1. Education--Case studies. I. Merino, Noël II. Gale Research Inc.
    LA21.E29 2014
    370--dc23
                                     2013030015

Contents

Chapter 3: Should Religion and Religious Ideas Be Part of Public Education?

Chapter 4: How Should the Education System Be Improved?

Why Consider Opposing Viewpoints?

> *"The only way in which a human being can make some approach to knowing the whole of a subject is by hearing what can be said about it by persons of every variety of opinion and studying all modes in which it can be looked at by every character of mind. No wise man ever acquired his wisdom in any mode but this."*
>
> *John Stuart Mill*

In our media-intensive culture it is not difficult to find differing opinions. Thousands of newspapers and magazines and dozens of radio and television talk shows resound with differing points of view. The difficulty lies in deciding which opinion to agree with and which "experts" seem the most credible. The more inundated we become with differing opinions and claims, the more essential it is to hone critical reading and thinking skills to evaluate these ideas. Opposing Viewpoints books address this problem directly by presenting stimulating debates that can be used to enhance and teach these skills. The varied opinions contained in each book examine many different aspects of a single issue. While examining these conveniently edited opposing views, readers can develop critical thinking skills such as the ability to compare and contrast authors' credibility, facts, argumentation styles, use of persuasive techniques, and other stylistic tools. In short, the Opposing Viewpoints Series is an ideal way to attain the higher-level thinking and reading skills so essential in a culture of diverse and contradictory opinions.

In addition to providing a tool for critical thinking, Opposing Viewpoints books challenge readers to question their own strongly held opinions and assumptions. Most people form their opinions on the basis of upbringing, peer pressure, and personal, cultural, or professional bias. By reading carefully balanced opposing views, readers must directly confront new ideas as well as the opinions of those with whom they disagree. This is not to simplistically argue that everyone who reads opposing views will—or should—change his or her opinion. Instead, the series enhances readers' understanding of their own views by encouraging confrontation with opposing ideas. Careful examination of others' views can lead to the readers' understanding of the logical inconsistencies in their own opinions, perspective on why they hold an opinion, and the consideration of the possibility that their opinion requires further evaluation.

Evaluating Other Opinions

To ensure that this type of examination occurs, Opposing Viewpoints books present all types of opinions. Prominent spokespeople on different sides of each issue as well as well-known professionals from many disciplines challenge the reader. An additional goal of the series is to provide a forum for other, less known, or even unpopular viewpoints. The opinion of an ordinary person who has had to make the decision to cut off life support from a terminally ill relative, for example, may be just as valuable and provide just as much insight as a medical ethicist's professional opinion. The editors have two additional purposes in including these less known views. One, the editors encourage readers to respect others' opinions—even when not enhanced by professional credibility. It is only by reading or listening to and objectively evaluating others' ideas that one can determine whether they are worthy of consideration. Two, the inclusion of such viewpoints encourages the important critical thinking skill of objectively evaluating an author's credentials and bias. This evaluation will illuminate an author's reasons for taking a particular stance on an issue and will aid in readers' evaluation of the author's ideas.

It is our hope that these books will give readers a deeper understanding of the issues debated and an appreciation of the complexity of even seemingly simple issues when good and honest people disagree. This awareness is particularly important in a democratic society such as ours in which people enter into public debate to determine the common good. Those with whom one disagrees should not be regarded as enemies but rather as people whose views deserve careful examination and may shed light on one's own.

Thomas Jefferson once said that "difference of opinion leads to inquiry, and inquiry to truth." Jefferson, a broadly educated man, argued that "if a nation expects to be ignorant and free . . . it expects what never was and never will be." As individuals and as a nation, it is imperative that we consider the opinions of others and examine them with skill and discernment. The Opposing Viewpoints Series is intended to help readers achieve this goal.

David L. Bender and Bruno Leone,
Founders

Introduction

> *"Separate educational facilities are inherently unequal."*
>
> Chief Justice Earl Warren,
> Brown v. Board of Education *(1954)*

The public school system in the United States of America is rooted in an attempt to bring equal education to all American children. The first major development in establishing public education focused on providing free schools to the poor in the nineteenth century. The second major development was in the twentieth century and aimed to desegregate schools and provide equal education to all Americans regardless of race. In both movements, the core principle of equal education for all emerged, forming the foundation of the public school system that exists today.

The American public school system has its origins in the nineteenth-century movement by several states to provide public funds for education. Prior to that, education had been a function of the family, church, or private entities that charged tuition. During the early nineteenth century, churches and charity organizations promoted free schooling for the poor. In Massachusetts, state legislators James G. Carter and Horace Mann led efforts to establish a system of public schooling in that state. In 1827, Massachusetts passed The Massachusetts Public School Act requiring towns to provide schools and teachers:

> Each town or district of 50 families must have a teacher of orthography, geography, reading, writing, English grammar, arithmetic and good behavior at least 6 months in a year. If of 100 families, there must be teachers to equal 18 months in a year. If 500 families, must equal 24 months in a year and must add the History of the United States, bookkeeping

by single entry, geometry, surveying, and algebra and must have a Master for Latin and Greek.[1]

In 1837, Massachusetts was the first state to establish a board of education, headed by Mann, establishing statewide standards. The advent of free public schooling was driven by the idea that poverty should not be a barrier to education.

By 1870, all states had free elementary schools and by the end of the nineteenth century, public high schools outnumbered private ones. By 1900, more than half the states had laws requiring school attendance until at least age fourteen. Despite progress in establishing schooling for all, schools in the early twentieth century were segregated by race. The US Supreme Court in 1896 had ruled that states were allowed to pass laws requiring racial segregation:

> Laws permitting, and even requiring, their separation in places where they are liable to be brought into contact do not necessarily imply the inferiority of either race to the other, and have been generally, if not universally, recognized as within the competency of the state legislatures in the exercise of their police power. The most common instance of this is connected with the establishment of separate schools for white and colored children, which has been held to be a valid exercise of the legislative power even by courts of States where the political rights of the colored race have been longest and most earnestly enforced.[2]

Thus, during the first half of the nineteenth century, all American students had access to education, but the schools were segregated by race.

The Civil Rights Movement of the mid-twentieth century brought to light the inequalities of segregation. In 1954 the Supreme Court repudiated its 1896 decision, holding in its landmark unanimous decision of *Brown v. Board of Education* that "in the field of public education, the doctrine of 'separate but equal' has no place. Separate educational facilities are inherently unequal."[3] The decision was not welcomed by all, especially by states in the South, and the process of desegregation was lengthy and violent at times. The decision did firmly establish, however, that all Americans were to be treated equally under the law when it came to education.

Despite the establishment of free public schools and the official abandonment of legal segregation, many public schools in America continue to have wide racial and socioeconomic disparities. A 2012 report by the Civil Rights Project contends that racial segregation in public schools continues over fifty years after the Court's decision in *Brown v. Board of Education*: "In spite of the dramatic suburbanization of nonwhite families, 80% of Latino students and 74% of black students attend majority nonwhite schools (50–100% minority), and 43% of Latinos and 38% of blacks attend intensely segregated schools (those with only 0–10% of white students) across the nation." Furthermore, schools are currently segregated by both race and income: "The typical black or Latino today attends school with almost double the share of low-income students in their schools than the typical white or Asian student."[4] Whether these trends undermine the foundational principles for public education is open to debate, but they do illustrate that despite efforts to bring equal education to all American children regardless of income or race, the demographics of public schools show continued segregation in both these spheres.

The mission to establish free public education for all in America is one that has been fraught with questions about the best way to bring education to a diverse nation of students. Students from all socioeconomic, racial, religious, and cultural backgrounds are served by the public school system. Efforts to meet their educational needs and the desires of their parents in a way that promotes equality inevitably create debate at both the national and local levels, prompting a variety of questions, the following of which appear as chapter titles in the current volume: What Is the State of Education in

America?, Are School-Choice Alternatives a Good Idea?, Should Religion and Religious Ideas Be Part of Public Education?, and How Should the Education System Be Improved?

A variety of answers to these questions regarding the current state of public education in America and the proposals for improving the system for all children are explored in *Opposing Viewpoints: Education*.

Notes

1. Quoted in David A. Copeland, *The Antebellum Era: Primary Documents on Events from 1820 to 1860*. Westport, CT: Greenwood Press, 2003.
2. *Plessy v. Ferguson*, 163 US 537 (1896).
3. *Brown v. Board of Education*, 347 US 483 (1954).
4. Gary Orfield, John Kucsera, and Genevieve Siegel-Hawley, "*E Pluribus* . . . Separation: Deepening Double Segregation for More Students," Civil Rights Project, September 2012. www.civilrightsproject.ucla.edu.

CHAPTER 1

What Is the State of Education in America?

Chapter Preface

According to the Gallup polling organization, most Americans are dissatisfied with the quality of education that students receive from kindergarten through grade twelve. A poll in August 2012 showed that 37 percent of Americans were somewhat dissatisfied and 16 percent completely dissatisfied, whereas 36 percent were somewhat satisfied and only 8 percent completely satisfied. When Americans were asked how much confidence they had in the public schools, only 11 percent said they had a great deal of confidence, and 28 percent reported very little confidence. When asked to rate public schools, only 5 percent of Americans said that public schools provide children with an excellent education. Thirty-two percent felt that public school education was good, but 42 percent said it was only fair, and 19 percent thought it was poor. Clearly, Americans differ in their assessment of the state of education in America.

In response to widespread dissatisfaction with education outcomes, Congress passed, and President George W. Bush signed, the No Child Left Behind Act (NCLB) in 2001. Among other requirements, NCLB requires all public schools that receive federal funding to administer yearly standardized tests and to give evidence of adequate yearly progress. The states are able to design their own tests and set their own benchmarks for defining and measuring yearly progress. Allowing the states control over education testing and goals is popular among those who want local control of education policy and less federal involvement; however, critics charge that without national standards, there is no reliable way to assess how students are doing from state to state, nor is there a way to ensure that one state's standards are not vastly lower than another state's standards.

When asked to poll Americans in August 2012 about how NCLB has impacted the education of public school students, the Gallup organization reported that only 16 percent of Americans said that it had made education better, whereas 29 percent thought that it had made public school education worse. When asked whether the federal government should be more involved in education, 39 percent of all adults said yes, and 42 percent of parents of school-aged children said yes. But 36 percent of all adults wanted less government involvement, similar to the 35 percent of parents of school-aged children who said the same. There is certainly a consensus that American public education can be improved, but assessments of problem areas and possible solutions vary widely, as the debate in this chapter shows.

"Only 6 percent of U.S. students per-form at the advanced-proficiency level in math, a share that lags behind kids in some 30 other countries."

American Students Perform Poorly Compared to Students in Other Countries

Amanda Ripley

In the following viewpoint, Amanda Ripley argues that educa-tion in the United States compares unfavorably with interna-tional levels. Ripley claims that even when comparing individual states to other countries, no US state comes out in the top twelve. Furthermore, she contends that researchers have found that even among the privileged, American students do not stand out among international groups. Ripley does aver that the relative success of education in Massachusetts is providing a template for education reform across the country.

Amanda Ripley writes for the Atlantic Monthly *and* Time *magazine and is the author of* The Smartest Kids in the World—and How They Got That Way.

As you read, consider the following questions:

1. According to the author, which two US states are ranked in the upper-middle tier when comparing math performance internationally?

2. What is the "diversity excuse" that parents give for America's low education ranking internationally, according to Ripley?

3. According to the author, which three other countries spend more than the United States does on elementary and secondary education?

Imagine for a moment that a rich, innovative company is looking to draft the best and brightest high-school grads from across the globe without regard to geography. Let's say this company's recruiter has a round-the-world plane ticket and just a few weeks to scout for talent. Where should he go?

The Quality of U.S. Education

Our hypothetical recruiter knows there's little sense in judging a nation like the United States by comparing it to, say, Finland. This is a big country, after all, and school quality varies dramatically from state to state. What he really wants to know is, should he visit Finland or Florida? Korea or Connecticut? Uruguay or Utah?

Stanford economist Eric Hanushek and two colleagues recently conducted an experiment to answer just such questions, ranking American states and foreign countries side by side. Like our recruiter, they looked specifically at the best and brightest in each place—the kids most likely to get good jobs in the future—using scores on standardized math tests as a proxy for educational achievement.

We've known for some time how this story ends nationwide: only 6 percent of U.S. students perform at the advanced-proficiency level in math, a share that lags behind kids in some 30 other countries, from the United Kingdom to Taiwan. But what happens when we break down the results? Do any individual U.S. states wind up near the top?

Incredibly, no. Even if we treat each state as its own country, not a single one makes it into the top dozen contenders on the list. The best performer is Massachusetts, ringing in at No. 17. Minnesota also makes it into the upper-middle tier, followed by Vermont, New Jersey, and Washington. And down it goes from there, all the way to Mississippi, whose students—by this measure at least—might as well be attending school in Thailand or Serbia.

Explaining Underperformance

Hanushek, who grew up outside Cleveland and graduated from the Air Force Academy in 1965, has the gentle voice and manner of [children's television personality] Mr. Rogers, but he has spent the past 40 years calmly butchering conventional wisdom on education. In study after study, he has demonstrated that our assumptions about what works are almost always wrong. More money does *not* tend to lead to better results; smaller class sizes do *not* tend to improve learning. "Historically," he says, "reporters call me [when] the editor asks, 'What is the other side of this story?'"

Over the years, as Hanushek has focused more on international comparisons, he has heard a variety of theories as to why U.S. students underperform so egregiously. When he started, the prevailing excuse was that the testing wasn't fair. Other countries were testing a more select group of students, while we were testing everyone. That is no longer true: due to better sampling techniques and other countries' decisions to educate more of their citizens, we're now generally comparing apples to apples.

These days, the theory Hanushek hears most often is what we might call the diversity excuse. When he runs into his neighbors at Palo Alto [California] coffee shops, they lament the condition of public schools overall, but are quick to exempt the schools their own kids attend. "In the litany of excuses, one explanation is always, 'We're a very heterogeneous society—all these immigrants are dragging us down. But *our* kids are doing fine,'" Hanushek says. This latest study was designed, in part, to test the diversity excuse.

To do this, Hanushek, along with Paul Peterson at Harvard and Ludger Woessmann at the University of Munich, looked at the American kids performing at the top of the charts on an international math test. (Math tests are easier to normalize across countries, regardless of language barriers; and math skills tend to better predict future earnings than other skills taught in high school.) Then, to get state-by-state data, they correlated the results of that international test with the results of the National Assessment of Educational Progress exam, which is given to a much larger sample in the U.S. and can be used to draw statewide conclusions.

Testing the Diversity Excuse

The international test Hanushek used for this study—the Programme for International Student Assessment, or PISA—is administered every three years to 15-year-olds in about 60 countries. Some experts love this test; others, like Tom Loveless at the Brookings Institution, criticize it as a poor judge of what schools are teaching. But despite his concerns about PISA, Loveless, who has read an advance version of Hanushek's study, agrees with its primary conclusion. "The United States does not do a good job of educating kids at the top," he says. "There's a long-standing attitude that, 'Well, smart kids can make it on their own. And after all, they're doing well. So why worry about them?'"

Of course, the fact that no U.S. state does very well compared with other rich nations does not necessarily disprove the diversity excuse: parents in Palo Alto could reasonably infer that California's poor ranking (in the bottom third, just

Student Achievement in Advanced Math

This three-page chart shows the percentage of students at an advanced level of math achievement in the fifty states and in countries participating in the 2006 Programme for International Student Assessment (PISA).

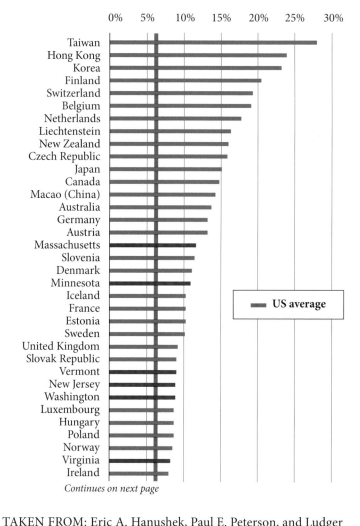

Continues on next page

TAKEN FROM: Eric A. Hanushek, Paul E. Peterson, and Ludger Woessmann, "Teaching Math to the Talented," *Education Next*, Winter 2011.

Student Achievement in Advanced Math (continued)

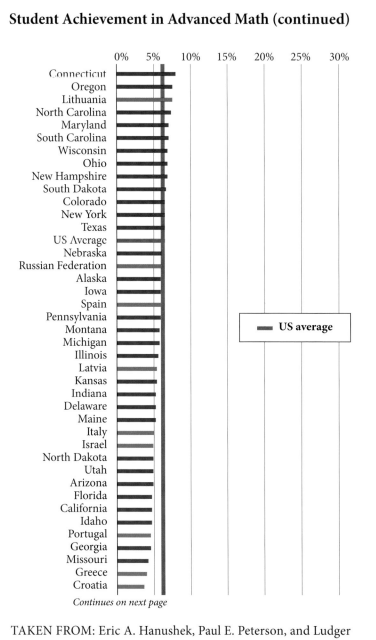

Continues on next page

TAKEN FROM: Eric A. Hanushek, Paul E. Peterson, and Ludger Woessmann, "Teaching Math to the Talented," *Education Next*, Winter 2011.

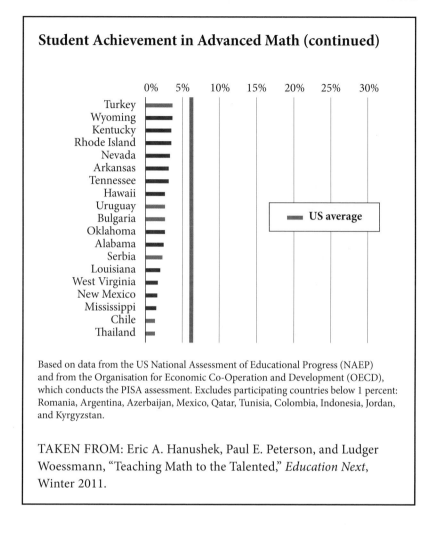

Student Achievement in Advanced Math (continued)

Based on data from the US National Assessment of Educational Progress (NAEP) and from the Organisation for Economic Co-Operation and Development (OECD), which conducts the PISA assessment. Excludes participating countries below 1 percent: Romania, Argentina, Azerbaijan, Mexico, Qatar, Tunisia, Colombia, Indonesia, Jordan, and Kyrgyzstan.

TAKEN FROM: Eric A. Hanushek, Paul E. Peterson, and Ludger Woessmann, "Teaching Math to the Talented," *Education Next*, Winter 2011.

above Portugal and below Italy) is a function of the state's large population of poor and/or immigrant children, and does not reflect their own kids' relatively well-off circumstances.

So Hanushek and his co-authors sliced the data more thinly still. They couldn't control for income, since students don't report their parents' salaries when they take these tests; but they could use reliable proxies. How would our states do if we looked just at the white kids performing at high levels—kids who are not, generally speaking, subject to language barriers or racial discrimination? Or if we looked just at kids with at least one college-educated parent?

As it turned out, even these relatively privileged students do not compete favorably with average students in other well-off countries. On a percentage basis, New York state has fewer high performers among white kids than Poland has among kids overall. In Illinois, the percentage of kids with a college-educated parent who are highly skilled at math is lower than the percentage of such kids among *all* students in Iceland, France, Estonia, and Sweden.

Parents in Palo Alto will always insist that their kids are the exception, of course. And researchers cannot compare small cities and towns around the globe—not yet, anyway. But Hanushek thinks the study significantly undercuts the diversity excuse. "People will find it quite shocking," he says, "that even our most-advantaged students are not all that competitive."

The Success in Massachusetts

Reading the list, one cannot help but thank God for Massachusetts, which offers the United States some shred of national dignity—a result echoed in other international tests. "If all American fourth- and eighth-grade kids did as well in math and science as they do in Massachusetts," writes the veteran education author Karin Chenoweth in her 2009 book, *How It's Being Done*, "we still wouldn't be in Singapore's league but we'd be giving Japan and Chinese Taipei a run for their money."

Is it because Massachusetts is so white? Or so immigrant-free? Or so rich? Not quite. Massachusetts is indeed slightly whiter and slightly better-off than the U.S. average. But in the late 1990s, it nonetheless lagged behind similar states—such as Connecticut and Maine—in nationwide tests of fourth- and eighth-graders. It was only after a decade of educational reforms that Massachusetts began to rank first in the nation.

What did Massachusetts do? Well, nothing that many countries (and industries) didn't do a long time ago. For example, Massachusetts made it harder to become a teacher, requiring newcomers to pass a basic literacy test before entering the classroom. (In the first year, more than a third of the new teachers failed the test.) The state also required students to pass a test before graduating from high school—a notion so heretical that it led to protests in which students burned state superintendent David Driscoll in effigy. To help tutor the kids who failed, the state moved money around to the places where it was needed most. "We had a system of standards and held people to it—adults and students," Driscoll says.

Massachusetts, in other words, began demanding meaningful outcomes from everyone in the school building. Obvious though it may seem, it's an idea that remains sacrilegious in many U.S. schools, despite the clumsy advances of No Child Left Behind.[1] Instead, we still fixate on inputs—such as how much money we are pouring into the system or how small our class sizes are—and wind up with little to show for it. Since the early 1970s, we've doubled the amount of money we spend per pupil nationwide, but our high-schoolers' reading and math scores have barely budged.

Per student, we now spend more than all but three other countries—Luxembourg, Switzerland, and Norway—on elementary and secondary education. And the list of countries that spend the most, notably, has little in common with the outcomes that Hanushek and his colleagues put into rank order. (The same holds true on the state level, where New York, one of the highest-spending states—it topped the list at $17,000 per pupil in 2008—still comes in behind 15 other states and 30 countries on Hanushek's list.)

---

1. The No Child Left Behind Act of 2001 requires individual states to set high educational standards and develop appropriate assessments to improve educational outcomes for students.

The Adoption of Common Standards

However haltingly, more states are finally beginning to follow the lead of Massachusetts. At least 35 states and the District of Columbia agreed this year [2010] to adopt common standards for what kids should know in math and language arts—standards informed in part by what kids in top-performing countries are learning. Still, all of the states, Massachusetts included, have a long way to go. Last year [2009], a study comparing standardized math tests given to third-graders in Massachusetts and Hong Kong found embarrassing disparities. Even at that early age, kids in Hong Kong were being asked more-demanding questions that required more-complex responses.

Meanwhile, a 2010 study of teacher-prep programs in 16 countries found a striking correlation between how well students did on international exams and how their future teachers performed on a math test. In the U.S., researchers tested nearly 3,300 teachers-to-be in 39 states. The results? Our future middle-school math teachers knew about as much math as their peers in Thailand and Oman—and nowhere near what future teachers in Taiwan and Singapore knew. Moreover, the results showed dramatic variation depending on the teacher-training program. Perhaps this should not be surprising: teachers cannot teach what they do not know, and to date, most have not been required to know very much math.

Early last year, President [Barack] Obama reminded Congress, "The countries that out-teach us today will out-compete us tomorrow." This September, Ontario Premier Dalton McGuinty, visiting a local school on the first day of classes, mentioned Obama's warning and smugly took note of the scoreboard: "Well," he said, "we are out-teaching them today."

Arne Duncan, Obama's education secretary, responded to the premier's trash-talking a few days later. "When I played professional basketball in Australia, that's the type of quote the coach would post on the bulletin board in the locker room," he declared during a speech in Toronto. And then his rejoinder came to a crashing halt. "In all seriousness," Duncan confessed, "Premier McGuinty spoke the truth."

> *"Among the 25 nations participating at 4th grade, the U.S. is sixth with an estimated 37% of its students proficient or better on the 2007 [National Assessment of Educational Progress]."*

American Students Perform Favorably Compared to Students in Other Countries

Gerald W. Bracey

In the following viewpoint, Gerald W. Bracey argues that statistics on educational performance show that the United States ranks higher than most nations. Bracey contends that although the United States has a few cities that do not rank very well, he denies that there is a crisis in education. Furthermore, Bracey claims that there is no significant correlation between the performance of students on tests and the level of innovation or economic success of a nation.

Gerald W. Bracey is a fellow at several educational think tanks, a frequently published commentator, and the author of several books on the topic of education, including Setting the

Gerald W. Bracey, "U.S. School Performance, Through a Glass Darkly (Again)," *Phi Delta Kappan*, vol. 90, no. 5, January 2009, pp. 386–387. Reprinted with permission of Phi Delta Kappa International, www.pdkintl.org. All rights reserved.

Record Straight: Responses to Misconceptions About Public Education in the U.S.

As you read, consider the following questions:

1. The author reports that the United States ranked in what place among forty-four countries in math proficiency at eighth grade?

2. What European country does Bracey say Chicago eighth graders fare better than in math proficiency?

3. Which three cities in the United States does the author say score higher "percent proficient" than the average Organisation for Economic Cooperation and Development nation?

I suppose we must expect gloomy predictions about schools from those who have vested interests in depicting them as ruinous, but we shouldn't expect to see such from a place like the American Institutes for Research (AIR). But that's what we get from AIR's Gary Phillips and John Dossey of Illinois State University, authors of *Counting on the Future: International Benchmarks for American School Districts*.

An Inaccurate Assessment

The report, like so many similar reports, begins with false premises and closes with an illogical conclusion. The premises are these:

> Large corporations locate their businesses in U.S. cities; foreign students attend U.S. schools; and U.S. businesses export goods and services to foreign nations. Large urban cities need to know how their students stack up against peers in the nations with which the U.S. does business. This is especially important for students in the fields of science, technology, engineering, and mathematics. The students in these fields will allow our future generation [sic] to remain technologically innovative and economically competitive.

It's hard to imagine a shorter paragraph containing more misinformation. Did BMW build a plant in South Carolina, Mercedes a plant in Alabama, and did Nissan move its U.S. headquarters to Tennessee because of these states' high math scores? Hardly. They built and moved [to these states] because they got enormous tax breaks, no unions, and cheaper labor.

Second, this report compares average scores in the U.S. and selected U.S. cities with average scores in other nations. Such comparisons tell us nothing. Reports such as AIR's concentrate on the supply side of skills and ignore the demand side. Does the market demand more scientists and engineers? Hardly. The U.S. has three new native-born or permanent-resident scientists and engineers for every new scientific and engineering position being created. What the market wants is cheap scientists and engineers, which is no doubt why 65% of new graduates leave science and engineering within two years.

Third, the recent Global Competitiveness Report 2008–2009 from the World Economic Forum (WEF) ranks the U.S. #1—again. Japan's kids were acing tests when *A Nation at Risk*[1] was published 25 years ago and they continued to ace tests even as that nation sank into 15 years of economic recession and stagnation. The link between test scores and a nation's economic health simply isn't there. Does anyone—anyone!—think low test scores created the current crisis? If so, it would have to be the low scores of business school graduates on ethics tests.

A Comparison of Nations

Phillips and Dossey use a linking technique that permits one to estimate how students from other nations would perform if they sat for our NAEP [National Assessment of Educational Progress] tests. The report first summarizes the U.S. generally

---

1. The 1983 report of President Ronald Reagan's National Commission on Excellence in Education that warned of America's failing schools and called for education reforms to boost student achievement.

Math Proficiency Worldwide

Comparison of the 2007 grade 4 National Assessment of Education Progress (NAEP) in mathematics for the United States and the 2003 grade 4 Trends in International Mathematics and Science Study (TIMSS) results for the percent at and above proficient, based on NAEP achievement levels projected onto the TIMSS scale

Percent at and above proficient

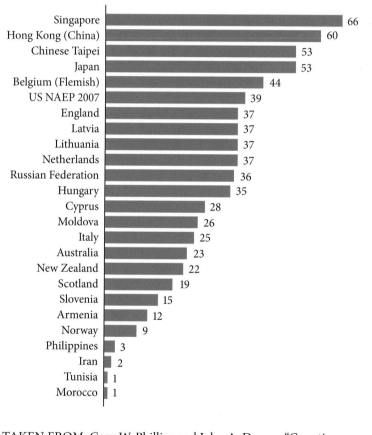

Country	Percent
Singapore	66
Hong Kong (China)	60
Chinese Taipei	53
Japan	53
Belgium (Flemish)	44
US NAEP 2007	39
England	37
Latvia	37
Lithuania	37
Netherlands	37
Russian Federation	36
Hungary	35
Cyprus	28
Moldova	26
Italy	25
Australia	23
New Zealand	22
Scotland	19
Slovenia	15
Armenia	12
Norway	9
Philippines	3
Iran	2
Tunisia	1
Morocco	1

TAKEN FROM: Gary W. Phillips and John A. Dossey, "Counting on the Future: International Benchmarks in Mathematics for American School Districts," American Institutes for Research, October 2008.

against other nations participating in the math segment of TIMSS [Trends in International Mathematics and Science Study]. Among the 25 nations participating at 4th grade, the U.S. is sixth with an estimated 37% of its students proficient or better on the 2007 NAEP. At 8th grade, the U.S. is 10th of 44 countries with 31% proficient. These rankings are the seeds of crisis?

Interestingly, only four nations have a majority of students proficient at the 4th-grade level, only five manage it at 8th grade. Singapore is tops in both grades with 66% proficient at 4th grade, 73% proficient at 8th grade. At 8th grade, 14 nations have 5% or fewer proficient. Norway has 9%, Italy 18%, Sweden 21%, Scotland and New Zealand 22%. These countries are generally considered "competitor nations." For four nations, including Saudi Arabia, the percent proficient rounds down to zero.

A Comparison of Cities

The report then considers results from the TIMSS nations held up against "large urban cities" that had participated in the 2007 NAEP. Some cities that are often cited as horrible examples take their lumps here. Chicago has only 16% proficient at 4th grade, 13% proficient at 8th grade—but that's better than Norway's 9%. Yet the WEF ranks Norway higher than high-scoring Taiwan (16th vs. 17th) and almost as high as Japan (9th), Korea (13th), and Hong Kong (11th). Only Singapore at 5th puts what looks like real daylight between itself and Norway. But it ranks behind Sweden in the WEF report, though 73% of its 8th graders are proficient compared to Sweden's 21%. The link between test scores and economies is simply not there.

For Los Angeles, the figures are 19% and 14% and for Atlanta, 20% and 11%. Cleveland and the District of Columbia make double digits only at 4th grade.

But Houston is almost at the median at 4th grade (28%) and above the median at 8th grade (21%). And New York City is at the median in 4th grade (34%) and above it at 8th grade (22%). And Boston scores 27% proficient at both grades. San Diego gets 35% of its 4th graders to the proficient level but falls to 24% at 8th grade.

Two cities that are often perceived as university towns, Austin and Charlotte, do even better. Charlotte finishes higher than the U.S. average with 44% proficient at 4th grade and 34% at 8th grade. This figure ranks it sixth among 25 nations at 4th grade and 10th among 44 at 8th grade. Austin has the same rankings, having 40% of 4th graders proficient and 34% of 8th graders. This means that at 4th grade, Austin and Charlotte are just behind Singapore, Hong Kong, Taiwan, Japan, and Flemish Belgium.

The Significance of Differences

The report examines how the cities stack up against the average of the nations. At 4th grade, Austin, Charlotte, San Diego, and the U.S. as a whole do significantly better than the TIMSS average. Houston and Boston do about the same, while Atlanta, Chicago, Cleveland, Los Angeles, and the District of Columbia do significantly worse.

At 8th grade, Austin, Boston, Charlotte, and the U.S. as a whole do significantly better than the international average. Houston, San Diego, and New York City do about the same. Atlanta, Chicago, Cleveland, Los Angeles, and the District of Columbia do significantly worse.

Keep in mind that these "significant" differences are purely statistical. We have no idea about any practical significance.

Well, you say, when we compare American cities against individual countries or the TIMSS average, we're including some nations whose percent proficient rounds to zero. Thus the report goes on to compare the percent proficient in the cities and the average for the industrialized nations of the Organisation for Economic Co-operation and Development (OECD).

At 4th grade, Charlotte, Austin, San Diego, and the U.S. as a whole score significantly better than the average OECD nation. Boston, Houston, and New York City score about the same, while the other five cities—Atlanta, Boston, Chicago, Cleveland, and the District of Columbia—scored lower. At 8th grade, no city outperforms the OECD average. Charlotte, Austin, and the U.S. as a whole perform as well, but the other cities are all below the OECD average.

An Illogical Conclusion

The report closes with the usual illogical conclusion that because our kids don't match Singapore's in math, "we are already at a competitive disadvantage." I don't think so. I've reported on how employers are emphasizing soft skills and college admissions officers put more weight on extracurricular activities than on SAT [Scholastic Aptitude Test] scores. Equally important, just as these "dark side" reports never consider the demand for skills, they never take into account cultural variables. Most people who do the dirty work in Singapore actually live in Malaysia. Many long-term "guest workers" in Singapore come from the Philippines and can't bring their families with them. Singapore is thus spared the efforts required to educate an economically diverse population.

In [the October 26, 2008, *Boston Globe*], Jay Mathews wrote, "the impression that our schools are losing out to the rest of the world, that we are not producing enough scientists and engineers, is a misunderstanding fueled by misleading statistics." True enough. AIR's statistics are in places misleading, but their worst flaw is that the authors misinterpret them.

"It's difficult to overstate how extensive a role the unions play in making America's schools what they are—and in preventing them from being something different."

Teachers' Unions Have Not Been Good for American Education

Terry M. Moe

In the following viewpoint, Terry M. Moe argues that the immense power of teachers' unions has led to poor public education. Moe claims that because the interests of the unions are different from—and at odds with—the interests of children, bad teachers are protected by a perversely organized system. Moe concludes, however, that the time is particularly ripe for change.

Terry M. Moe is a senior fellow at the Hoover Institution and a member of the institution's Koret Task Force on K–12 Education; he is the William Bennett Munro Professor of Political Science at Stanford University and the author of Special Interest: Teachers Unions and America's Public Schools.

Terry M. Moe, "The Staggering Power of the Teachers' Unions," *Hoover Digest*, no. 3, July 13, 2011. *Special Interest: Teachers Unions and America's Public Schools*, by Terry M. Moe (Brookings Institute Press, 2011); Copyright © 2011 The Brookings Institute. All rights reserved. Reproduced by permission.

As you read, consider the following questions:

1. According to the author, how much does New York City spend each year on salary and benefits for teachers who have been removed from classrooms?

2. During what two decades, according to Moe, did most teachers in the United States join unions?

3. What three examples does the author give in support of his claim that changes wrought by technology will undermine union power?

Janet Archer painted watercolors. Gordon Russell planned trips to Alaska and Cape Cod. Others did crossword puzzles, read books, played chess, practiced ballet moves, argued with one another, and otherwise tried to fill up the time. The place was New York City. The year was 2009. And these were public school teachers passing a typical day in one of the city's Rubber Rooms—Temporary Reassignment Centers—where teachers were housed when they were considered so unsuited to teaching that they needed to be kept out of the classroom, away from the city's children.

The Union Defended Bad Teachers

There were more than seven hundred teachers in New York City's Rubber Rooms that year. Each school day they went to "work." They arrived in the morning at exactly the same hour as other city teachers, and they left at exactly the same hour in the afternoon. They got paid a full salary. They received full benefits, as well as all the usual vacation days, and they had their summers off. Just like real teachers. Except they didn't teach.

All of this cost the city between $35 million and $65 million a year for salary and benefits alone, depending on who was doing the estimating. And the total costs were even greater, for the district hired substitutes to teach their classes, rented space for the Rubber Rooms, and forked out half a million dollars annually for security guards to keep the teachers safe (mainly from one another, as tensions ran high in these places). At a time when New York City was desperate for money to fund its schools, it was spending a fortune every year for seven-hundred-plus teachers to stare at the walls.

Mayor Michael Bloomberg and Chancellor Joel Klein wanted to move bad teachers out of the system and off the payroll. But they couldn't. While most of their teachers were doing a good job in the classroom, the problem was that all teachers—even the incompetent and the dangerous—were protected by state tenure laws, by restrictive collective bargaining contracts, and by the local teachers' union, the United Federation of Teachers (UFT), which was the power behind the laws and the contracts and the legal defender of each and every teacher whose job was in trouble.

With such a big defensive line, teachers who were merely mediocre could not be touched. So Bloomberg and Klein chose to remove just the more egregious cases and send them to Rubber Rooms. But even these teachers stayed on the payroll—for a long time. They didn't leave; they didn't give up; and because the legal procedures were so thickly woven and offered union lawyers so much to work with, it took from two to five years just to resolve the typical case.

Undermining Education

Sometimes it seems that public education operates in a parallel universe, in which what is obviously perverse and debilitating for the organization of schools has become normal and expected. The purpose of the American public school system is to educate children. And because this is so, everything about the public schools—how they are staffed, how they are funded, and more generally how they are organized to do their work—should be decided with the best interests of children in mind. But this isn't what happens. Not even remotely.

The New York City school district is not organized to provide the best possible education to its children. As things now stand, it can't be. Why? If we could view the district's entire organization, we would doubtless find many reasons. But when it comes to bad teachers alone, the district is wasting millions of dollars because the rules it is required to follow in operating the schools—rules that are embedded in the local collective bargaining contract and state law—prevent it from quickly, easily, and inexpensively removing these teachers from the classroom. Getting bad teachers out of the classroom is essential if kids are to be educated effectively. Yet the formal rules prevent it.

These rules are part of the organization of New York City's schools. The district is literally *organized* to protect bad teachers and to undermine the efforts of leaders to ensure teacher quality. It is also *organized* to require that huge amounts of money be wasted on endless, unnecessary procedures. These undesirable outcomes do not happen by accident. They happen by design.

New York may seem unusual. Its dimensions dwarf those of the typical American school district, and its organizational perversities may be extreme as well. But the kind of problem I discuss here is quite common. Almost everywhere, in districts throughout the nation, America's public schools are typically not organized to provide the nation's children with the highest quality education.

Rules That Protect Bad Teachers

One example: salary schedules that pay teachers based on their seniority and formal credits and have nothing whatever to do with whether their students are learning anything. Another example: rules that give senior teachers their choice of jobs and make it impossible for districts to allocate teachers where they can do the greatest good for kids. Another example: rules that require districts to lay off teachers (in times of reduced revenues or enrollments, say) in reverse order of seniority, thus ensuring that excellent teachers will be automatically fired if they happen to have little seniority and that lousy teachers will be automatically retained if they happen to have lots of seniority.

These sorts of rules are common. But who in their right mind, if they were organizing the schools for the benefit of children, would organize them in this way? No one would. Yet the schools do get organized in this way. The examples I've given are the tip of a very large iceberg. As a result, even the most obvious steps toward better education are difficult, if not impossible, to take.

Researchers have long known, for example, that when a student is fortunate enough to have a teacher near the high end of the quality distribution rather than a teacher near the low end, the impact amounts to an entire year's worth of additional learning. Teacher quality makes an enormous difference. Indeed, even if the quality variation across teachers is less stark, the consequences for kids can still be profound. As researchers Eric Hanushek and Steven Rivkin report, if students had good teachers rather than merely average teachers for four or five years in a row, "the increased learning would be sufficient to close entirely the average gap between a typical low-income student receiving a free or reduced-price lunch and the average student who is not receiving free or reduced-price lunches." In other words, it would eliminate the achievement gap that this nation has struggled to overcome for decades. Good teachers matter, and they matter a lot. Yet our school system is organized to make it virtually impossible to get bad teachers out of the classroom, bases key personnel decisions on seniority rather than expertise, and in countless other ways erects obstacles to providing children with the best possible teachers.

The Influence of Teachers' Unions

Ineffective organization has long been an open secret. *A Nation at Risk* [the Ronald Reagan administration's study of the status of American education] warned in 1983 of a "rising tide of mediocrity" in America's schools—leading to a frenzied era of nonstop reforms that, it was hoped, would bring dramatic improvement. But today the facts show that this dramatic improvement hasn't happened, and that bold reforms are still needed to turn the schools around. The most intensive period of school reform in the nation's history has largely been a failure. So we now have two questions to ponder. To the first, which asks why the public schools are burdened by ineffective organization, we can add a second: why has the reform movement, which for a quarter century has been dedicated to bringing effective organization to the nation's schools, failed to do that? The answer to both questions, I argue, is much the same: these problems are largely due to the power of the teachers' unions.

It might seem that the teachers' unions would play a limited role in public education: fighting for better pay and working conditions for their members, but otherwise having little impact on the structure and performance of the public schools more generally. Yet nothing could be further from the truth. The teachers' unions have more influence on the public schools than any other group in American society.

Their influence takes two forms. They shape the schools from the bottom up, through collective bargaining activities so broad in scope that virtually every aspect of school organization bears the distinctive imprint of union design. They also shape the schools from the top down, through political activities that give them unrivaled influence over the laws and regulations imposed on public education by government, and that allow them to block or weaken governmental reforms they find threatening. In combining bottom-up and top-down in-

The Monopoly of Unions

Since public schools already enjoy a monopoly on nearly $600 billion in annual government education spending, the chief way in which the NEA [National Education Association] and AFT [American Federation of Teachers] minimize competition is by lobbying elected officials to maintain that monopoly—opposing policies such as charter schools, vouchers, and education tax credits that give families easier access to nonunion schooling . . . Union political contributions at the federal level are substantial. In fact, if the NEA and AFT are taken together (not unreasonable, given that they overwhelmingly support the same party and pursue a similar agenda), they constitute the most generous source of federal political donations over the past 20 years. According to a ranking by the Center for Responsive Politics (2009), the NEA and AFT together have spent $56 million on federal political contributions since 1989, roughly as much as [oil giants] Chevron, Exxon Mobil, the NRA [National Rifle Association], and [aeronautics leader] Lockheed Martin combined.

Andrew J. Coulson,
Cato Journal, *Winter 2010.*

fluence, and in combining them as potently as they do, the teachers' unions are unique among all actors in the educational arena.

The Rise of Union Power

It's difficult to overstate how extensive a role the unions play in making America's schools what they are—and in preventing them from being something different.

Before the 1960s, the power holders in America's public school system were the administrative professionals charged with running it, as well as the local school boards who appointed them. Teachers had little power, and they were unorganized aside from their widespread membership in the National Education Association (NEA), which was a professional organization controlled by administrators. In the 1960s, however, states began to adopt laws that for the first time promoted collective bargaining for public employees. When the American Federation of Teachers (AFT) launched a campaign to organize the nation's teachers into unions, the NEA turned itself into a labor union (and eventually kicked out the administrators) to compete, and the battle was on in thousands of school districts. By the time the dust settled in the early 1980s, virtually all districts of any size (outside the South) were successfully organized, collective bargaining was the norm, and the teachers' unions reigned supreme as the most powerful force in American education.

This transformation—the rise of union power—created what was essentially a new system of public education. This new system has now been in equilibrium for roughly thirty years, and throughout this time it has been vigorously protected—and stabilized—by the very union power that created it.

The Political Power of the Unions

The trademark of this new system is not just that the teachers' unions are pre-eminently powerful. It is also that they *use* their power to promote their own special interests—and *to make the organization of schooling a reflection of those interests*. They say, of course, that what is good for teachers is good for kids. But the simple fact is that they are not in the business of representing kids. They are unions. They represent the job-related interests of their *members*, and these interests are *not the same* as the interests of children.

Some things are obvious. It is not good for children that ineffective teachers cannot be removed from the classroom. It is not good for children that teachers cannot be assigned to the classrooms where they are needed most. It is not good for children that excellent young teachers get laid off before mediocre colleagues with more seniority. Yet the unions fight to see that schools are organized in these ways.

And there's more. The organization of schooling goes beyond the personnel rules of collective-bargaining contracts to include all the formal components of the school system: accountability, choice, funding, class size, special education, and virtually anything else policymakers deem relevant. These matters are subject to the authority of state and national governments, where they are fought out in the political process— and decisions are heavily determined by political power.

Here the unions' great strength as political organizations comes into play. The NEA and the AFT, with more than four million members between them, are by far the most powerful groups in the politics of education. They wield astounding sums of money, year after year, for campaign contributions and lobbying. They have armies of well-educated activists in every political district. They can orchestrate well-financed public-relations and media campaigns any time they want, on any topic or candidate. And they have supremely well-developed organizational apparatuses that blanket the country.

They don't always get their way on public policy, of course. The American system of checks and balances makes that impossible. But these same checks and balances also ensure that *blocking* new laws is much easier than getting them passed, and this is how the teachers' unions have used their power to great effect: not by getting the policies they want, but by stopping or weakening the policies they *don't* want—and thus preventing true education reform.

The Chance for Change

From the beginning of the reform era, reformers have focused on the problem of ineffective schools, and thus on fixing the schools themselves. Yet they have failed to resolve this problem because there is another problem—the problem of union power—that is more fundamental, and has prevented them from fixing the schools in ways that make sense and have real promise. If our nation ever hopes to transform the public schools, this problem of union power must be recognized for what it is. And it must be resolved.

But can it be resolved? This is the pivotal question for the future of American education. The answer, I believe, is yes—although major change may take decades.

In normal times, reformers who try to change the system or its underlying power structure will almost always lose. This is the Catch-22 of power: if you try to weaken powerful groups, they will normally be able to use their power to stop you. Yet, fortunately for the nation, *these are not normal times.* American education stands at what political scientists would call a critical juncture. Because of a largely accidental and quite abnormal confluence of events, the stars are lining up in a way that makes major change possible, and in fact will drive it forward. Two separate dynamics are at work.

Two Dynamics Supporting Change

The first is arising "endogenously"—that is, within the education system and its politics. More than at any other time in modern history, the teachers' unions are on the defensive: blamed for obstructing reform, defending bad teachers, imposing seniority rules, and in general, using their power to promote their own interests rather than the interests of kids and effective organization. And open criticism is coming not just from conservatives anymore. It is also coming from liberals, moderates, and Democrats. Key constituencies have become fed up. Fed up with perpetually abysmal schools for disadvantaged kids. Fed up with the party's perpetual impotence with regard to reform. Fed up with what Jonathan Alter of *Newsweek* has called the "stranglehold of the teachers' unions on the Democratic Party." The demand is palpable for the party to free itself to pursue serious education reform in the best interests of children, especially those who need it the most.

But the shifting political tides *will not be enough* to bring about major education reform. Absent some other dynamic, the unions will remain very powerful, with over four million members, tons of money, countless activists, and all their other weapons still intact. Their Democratic allies will allow reform to go only so far before pulling up short. Luckily, another dynamic *is* at work. This one is "exogenous"—arising entirely outside the educational and political systems—and will ultimately dovetail nicely with the political trends that are running against the unions. I'm speaking about the revolution in information technology, one of the most profoundly influential forces ever to hit this planet. It is fast transforming the fundamentals of human society, from how people communicate and interact to how they collect information, gain knowledge, and transact business. There is no doubt that it has the capacity to transform the way children learn, and that it will ultimately revolutionize education systems all around the world, including our own.

The specific kinds of changes wrought by technology— among them the massive substitution of technology for labor, the growing irrelevance of geography for teaching (which means that teachers can be anywhere, and no longer need to be concentrated in districts), and the huge expansion in attractive alternatives to the regular (unionized) public schools—are destined to undermine the very foundations of union power and make it much more difficult for them to block reform and impose their special interests through politics. This will lay the groundwork, over a period of decades, for truly massive reforms—and for the rise of a new system that is much more responsive to children's needs and much better organized to provide the quality education they deserve.

"There is no strong evidence that unions ... [are] at 'the heart' of our education problems."

Bipartisan, But Unfounded: The Assault on Teachers' Unions

Richard D. Kahlenberg

In the following viewpoint, Richard D. Kahlenberg argues that the attack on teachers' unions is unwarranted. Kahlenberg claims that collective bargaining is important for democracy and important for education, arguing that educators' interests align more closely with students' interests than other groups. He concludes that teachers' unions can help to bring about educational reform, and he contends that the general public strongly supports the collective bargaining rights of public employees.

Richard D. Kahlenberg is a senior fellow at the Century Foundation and coauthor of Why Labor Organizing Should Be a Civil Right: Rebuilding a Middle-Class Democracy by Enhancing Worker Voice.

Richard D. Kahlenberg, "Bipartisan, But Unfounded: The Assault on Teachers' Unions," *American Educator*, vol. 35, no. 4, Winter 2011–2012, pp. 14–18. Copyright © 2012 by the American Educator. All rights reserved. Reproduced by permission.

As you read, consider the following questions:

1. Kahlenberg argues that collective bargaining not only advances individual interests but also works to balance out the forces of what two entities?

2. Which six states does the author identify as having long forbidden collective bargaining for teachers?

3. What percentage of Americans oppose ending collective bargaining for public sector employees, according to a poll cited by Kahlenberg?

Teachers' unions are under unprecedented bipartisan attack. The drumbeat is relentless, from governors in Wisconsin and Ohio to the film directors of *Waiting for "Superman"* and *The Lottery*; from new lobbying groups like Michelle Rhee's StudentsFirst and Wall Street's Democrats for Education Reform to political columnists such as Jonathan Alter and George Will; from new books like political scientist Terry Moe's *Special Interest* and entrepreneurial writer Steven Brill's *Class Warfare* to even, at times, members of the Obama administration. The consistent message is that teachers' unions are the central impediment to educational progress in the United States.

Part of the assault is unsurprising given its partisan origins. Republicans have long been critical, going back to at least 1996, when presidential candidate Bob Dole scolded teachers' unions: "If education were a war, you would be losing it. If it were a business, you would be driving it into bankruptcy. If it were a patient, it would be dying." If you're a Republican who wants to win elections, going after teachers' unions makes parochial sense. According to Terry Moe, the National Education Association (NEA) and the American Federation of Teachers (AFT) gave 95 percent of their contributions to Democrats in federal elections between 1989 and 2010.[1] The nakedly partisan nature of Wisconsin Governor

Scott Walker's attack on public sector collective bargaining was exposed when he exempted from his legislation two unions that supported him politically: one representing police officers and the other representing firefighters.

What's new and particularly disturbing is that partisan Republicans are now joined by many liberals and Democrats in attacking teachers' unions. Davis Guggenheim, an avowed liberal who directed Al Gore's anti–global warming documentary *An Inconvenient Truth* and Barack Obama's convention biopic, was behind *Waiting for "Superman."* Normally liberal *New York Times* columnist Nicholas Kristof regularly attacks teachers' unions, as does Steven Brill, who contributed to the campaigns of Hillary Clinton and Barack Obama, yet compares teachers' union leaders to Saddam Hussein loyalists and South African apartheid officials. A string of current and former Democratic school superintendents (including New York City's Joel Klein and San Diego's Alan Bersin) have blamed unions for education's woes. Even President Obama strongly supports nonunionized charter schools and famously applauded the firing of every single teacher in Central Falls, Rhode Island.

The litany of complaints about teachers' unions is familiar. They make it "virtually impossible to get bad teachers out of the classroom," says Moe.[2] Critics claim they oppose school choice, oppose merit pay, and oppose efforts to have excellent teachers "assigned" to high-poverty schools where they are needed most.

Growing Democratic support of these criticisms has emboldened conservatives to go even further and call for the complete abolition of collective bargaining for teachers a half-century after it started.[3] Conservative education professor Jay Greene pines for a "return to the pre-collective bargaining era."[4] Teachers' unions "are at the heart" of our education problems, Moe says.[5] "As long as the teachers' unions remain powerful," he writes, the "basic requirements" of educational success "cannot be met."[6] The idea that policymakers can work with "reform" union leaders is, in his view, "completely wrong-headed,"[7] "fanciful and misguided."[8]

Critics suggest that collective bargaining for teachers is stacked, even undemocratic. Unlike the case of the private sector, where management and labor go head-to-head with clearly distinct interests, they say, in the case of teachers, powerful unions are actively involved in electing school board members, essentially helping pick the management team. Moreover, when collective bargaining covers education policy areas—such as class size or discipline codes—the public is shut out from the negotiations, they assert. Along the way, the interests of adults in the system are served, but not the interests of children, these critics suggest.

Criticisms Abound, Evidence Does Not

The critics' contentions, which I'll sum up as collective bargaining and teachers' unions being undemocratic and bad for schoolchildren, have no real empirical support. Democratic societies throughout the world recognize the basic right of employees to band together to pursue their interests and secure a decent standard of living, whether in the private or public sector. Article 23 of the 1948 Universal Declaration of Human Rights provides not only that workers should be shielded from discrimination but also that "everyone has the right to form and to join trade unions for the protection of his interests."[9]

Collective bargaining is important in a democracy, not only to advance individual interests, but to give unions the power to serve as a countervailing force against big business and big government. Citing the struggle of Polish workers against the Communist regime, Ronald Reagan declared in a Labor Day speech in 1980: "Where free unions and collective bargaining are forbidden, freedom is lost."[10]

In the United States, 35 states and the District of Columbia have collective bargaining by statute or by state constitution for public school teachers; the rest explicitly prohibit it, are silent on the matter, or allow the decision to be made at the local level.[11] It is no accident that the states that either prohibit collective bargaining for teachers, or by tradition have never had it, are mostly in the Deep South, the region of the country historically most hostile to extending democratic citizenship to all Americans.

The argument that collective bargaining is undemocratic fails to recognize that in a democracy, school boards are ultimately accountable to all voters—not just teachers, who often live and vote outside the district in which they teach, and who in any event represent a small share of total voters. Union endorsements matter in school board elections, but so do the interests of general taxpayers, parents, and everyone else who makes up the community. If school board members toe a teachers' union line that is unpopular with voters, those officials can be thrown out in the next election.

The title of Moe's most recent book, *Special Interest: Teachers Unions and America's Public Schools*, invokes a term historically applied to wealthy and powerful entities such as oil companies, tobacco interests, and gun manufacturers, whose narrow interests are recognized as often colliding with the more general public interest in such matters as clean water, good health, and public safety. Do rank-and-file teachers, who educate American schoolchildren and earn about $54,000 on average, really fall into the same category?

Former AFT President Albert Shanker long ago demonstrated that it was possible to be a strong union supporter and an education reformer, a tradition carried on today by President Randi Weingarten. Local unions are sometimes resistant to necessary change, but the picture painted by critics of unions is sorely outdated. Unions today support school choice within the public school system, but oppose private school vouchers that might further Balkanize the nation's students. Unions in New York City, Pittsburgh, and elsewhere favor teacher merit pay so long as it includes school-wide gains to reward effort while also encouraging cooperation among teachers. While unions disfavor plans to allow administrators to "allocate" teachers to high-poverty schools against their will (a policy that is reminiscent of forced student assignment for racial balance during the days of busing), both the NEA and the AFT favor paying teachers bonuses to attract them to high-poverty schools.

On the issue that arouses the most controversy, getting rid of bad educators, many teachers' unions today also favor weeding out those who are not up to the job, *not* based strictly on test scores or the subjective judgment of principals, but through multiple measures of performance, including "peer review" plans. In peer review, expert teachers come into a school and work with struggling educators; many of those educators improve, but when the expert teachers do not see sufficient improvement, they recommend termination (and the final decision rests with the superintendent and/or school board). The average fifth-grade teacher has a powerful self-interest in getting rid of an incompetent fourth-grade colleague, which is part of why peer review programs in places like Toledo, Ohio, and Montgomery County, Maryland, have resulted in increases in teacher terminations compared with previous systems in which administrators were in charge. In Montgomery County, for example, administrators dismissed just one teacher due to performance issues between 1994 and 1999, but during the first four years of the district's peer review program, 177 teachers were dismissed, were not renewed, or resigned.[12]

Moreover, there is no strong evidence that unions reduce overall educational outcomes or are, as Moe and other critics suggest, at "the heart" of our education problems. If collective bargaining were really a terrible practice for education, we would see stellar results in the grand experiments without it: the American South and the charter school arena. Why aren't the states that have long forbidden collective bargaining for teachers—Georgia, Mississippi, North Carolina, South Carolina, Texas, and Virginia—at the top of the educational heap? Why did the nation's most comprehensive study of charter schools (88 percent of which are nonunion), conducted by Stanford University researchers and sponsored by pro-charter foundations, conclude that charters outperformed regular public schools only 17 percent of the time, and actually did significantly worse 37 percent of the time?[13] Why, instead, do we see states like Massachusetts, and countries like Finland, both with strong teachers' unions, leading the pack?

Union critics like Moe reply, reasonably enough, that the South suffers from lots of other impediments to high achievement, such as higher levels of poverty, a history of segregation, and lower levels of school spending. Well, yes, but this response begs a question: If factors like poverty and segregation matter a great deal more to student achievement than the existence of collective bargaining, why not focus on those issues instead of claiming that the ability of teachers to band together and pursue their interests is the central problem in American education? Moreover, a 2002 review of 17 studies by researcher Robert Carini finds that when demographic factors *are* carefully controlled for, "unionism leads to modestly higher standardized achievement test scores."[14]

Critics of unions point out that teacher interests "are *not the same* as the interests of children."[15] That's certainly true, but who are the selfless adults who think only about kids? For-profit charter school operators whose allegiance is to shareholders? Principals who send troublemakers back into the classroom because they don't want school suspension numbers to look bad? Superintendents who sometimes junk promising reforms instituted by predecessors because they cannot personally take credit? Mayors who must balance the need to invest in kids against the strong desire of many voters to hold down taxes?

Do the hedge fund billionaires who bankroll charter schools have only the interests of children at heart? Might not it be in the self-interest of very wealthy individuals to suggest that expensive efforts at reducing poverty aren't necessary, and that a nonunion teaching environment will do the trick? When hedge fund managers argue that their income should be taxed at a 15 percent marginal rate, they limit government revenue and squeeze funds for a number of public pursuits, including schools. Is that putting the interests of kids ahead of adults, as the reformers suggest we should always do? Moreover, is the bias of Wall Street—that deregulation is good and unions distort markets—really beneficial for low-income children? Why aren't union critics more skeptical of deregulation in education, given that the deregulation of banking, also supported by Wall Street, wreaked havoc on the economy? And is the antipathy of hedge fund managers toward organized labor generally in the interests of poor and working-class students, whose parents can't make ends meet in part because organized labor has been eviscerated in the United States over the past half-century?

On many of the big educational issues—including levels of investment in education—the interests of educators who are in the classroom day in and day out do align nicely with the interests of the children they teach. Unlike the banks that want government money to cover for their reckless lending, teachers want money for school supplies and to reduce overcrowded classes. Yes, teachers have an interest in being well compensated, but presumably kids benefit too when higher salaries attract more talented educators than might otherwise apply.

Overall, as journalist Jonathan Chait has noted, politicians, who have short-term horizons, are prone to underinvesting in education, and teachers' unions "provide a natural bulwark" against that tendency.[16] Because most voters don't have kids in the public school system, parents with children in public schools need political allies. The fact that teachers have, by joining together, achieved some power in the political process surely helps explain why the United States does a better job of investing in education than preventing poverty. The child poverty rate in the United States is 21.6 percent, the fifth highest among 40 Organisation for Economic Co-operation and Development (OECD) nations. Only Turkey, Romania, Mexico, and Israel have higher child poverty rates. Put differently, we're in the bottom eighth in preventing child poverty.[17] By contrast, when the interests of children are directly connected with the interests of teachers—as they are on the question of public education spending—the United States ranks close to the top third. Among 39 OECD nations, the United States ranks 15th in spending on primary and secondary education as a percentage of gross domestic product.[18]

Moreover, the United States would probably rank even worse on the poverty score were it not for the influence of teachers' unions and the American labor movement generally. Education reformers like Michelle Rhee have adopted the mantra that poverty is just an "excuse" for low performance, blithely dismissing decades of evidence finding that socioeconomic status is by far the biggest predictor of academic achievement. If we could just get the unions to agree to stop protecting bad teachers and allow great teachers to be paid more, Rhee says, we could make all the difference in education. The narrative is attractive because it indeed would be wonderful if student poverty and economic school segregation didn't matter, and if heroic teachers could consistently overcome the odds for students. But educators like Albert Shanker, the head of the AFT from 1974–1997, knew better. He believed strongly that teachers' unions should be affiliated with the AFL-CIO, in part because teachers could do a much better job of educating students if educators were part of a coalition that fought to reduce income inequality and to improve housing and health care for children. Teachers know they will be more effective if children have full stomachs and proper eyeglasses, which is a central reason why the AFT remains an active part of the broader labor movement in trying to help rebuild the middle class.

While many divide the world between teachers' unions and reformers, the truth is that unions have long advocated a number of genuine reforms—inside and outside the classroom—that can have a sustained impact on reducing the achievement gap. They back early childhood education programs that blunt the impact of poverty and have been shown to have long-lasting effects on student outcomes. They back common academic standards of the type used by many of our successful international competitors. And in places like La Crosse, Wisconsin; Louisville, Kentucky; and Raleigh, North Carolina; teachers have backed public school choice policies that reduce concentrations of school poverty, thereby placing more low-income students in middle-class schools and increasing their chances of success.

Moreover, by democratizing education and giving teachers voice, unions can strengthen schools by tapping into the promising ideas teachers have for reform. At the same time, giving teachers greater voice reduces frustration and turnover. It is well documented that while teacher turnover is high in regular public schools, it is even higher in the largely nonunionized charter sector. As researchers David Stuit and Thomas M. Smith have found: "The odds of a charter school teacher leaving the profession versus staying in the same school were 130 percent greater than those of a traditional public school teacher. Similarly, the odds of a charter school teacher moving to another school were 76 percent greater."[19] Some charter advocates have tried to spin the higher turnover rates as a virtue, but according to researcher Gary Miron, "attrition from the removal of ineffective teachers—a potential plus of charters—explains only a small portion of the annual exodus."[20]

Critics of unions also fail to understand that the union leaders benefit immeasurably from the insights of their members. In a much-discussed twist in his book *Class Warfare*, Steven Brill suggests that Randi Weingarten be appointed chancellor of New York City's public schools: once liberated from her obligation to represent teachers, she could use her savvy and smarts to improve education. But this suggestion misses the crucial point that much of a union leader's strength comes from the fact that she or he constantly interacts with teachers and learns from them how education reform theories actually work in practice.

Other union critics also try, unfairly, to drive a wedge between teachers and their elected union leaders. Columnist Jonathan Alter, for example, claims: "It's very, very important to hold two contradictory ideas in your head at the same time. Teachers are great, a national treasure. Teachers' unions are, generally speaking, a menace and an impediment to reform."[21] Interestingly, Moe, citing extensive polling data, concludes that his fellow critics like Alter are wrong on this matter. Moe finds that among teachers, "virtually all union members, whether Democrat or Republican, see their membership in the local as entirely voluntary and are highly satisfied with what they are getting."[22] In a 2009 survey, 80 percent of teachers agreed that "without collective bargaining, the working conditions and salaries of teachers would be much worse," and 82 percent agreed that "without a union, teachers would be vulnerable to school politics or administrators who abuse their power."[23]

Finally, teachers' unions, more than any other organizations, preserve the American system of public schools against privatization proposals. Other groups also oppose private school vouchers—including those advocating on behalf of civil liberties and civil rights, school boards associations, and the like. But only teachers' unions have the political muscle and sophistication to stop widespread privatization. Today, vouchers and similar schemes serve one-third of 1 percent of the American school population. This fact infuriates union critics, including those who see large profit potential in privatization, and delights a majority of the American public.

Most of the public also supports collective bargaining for teachers and other public employees. A *USA Today*/Gallup survey found that by 61 to 33 percent, Americans oppose ending collective bargaining for public sector employees.[24] An NBC News/*Wall Street Journal* poll found that while most Americans want public employees to pay more for retirement benefits and health care, 77 percent said unionized state and municipal employees should have the same rights as union members who work in the private sector.[25] In November, Ohio voters overwhelmingly supported the collective bargaining rights of public employees, voting to repeal an antibargaining law by a margin of 61 to 39 percent.

The public is right on this question. Teachers should not have to go back to the pre-collective bargaining era, when they engaged in what Shanker called "collective begging."[26] Educators were very poorly compensated; in New York City, they were paid less than those washing cars for a living. Teachers were subject to the whims of often autocratic principals and could be fired for joining a union.

Many states are facing dire budget crises, and unions need to be smart about advocating strategies that keep fiscal concerns in mind. That means moving beyond traditional efforts to pour more money into high-poverty schools. Magnet schools, which give low-income students a chance to be educated in a middle-class environment, are an especially promising investment. But this kind of engagement in education policy involves moving in a direction opposite from the one advocated by Michelle Rhee, Governor Scott Walker, and other Democratic and Republican union critics.

As Shanker noted years ago, restricting bargaining to the issue of wages (as many states are now trying to do) is a clever trap in which critics can suggest that teachers care only about money. Collective bargaining should be broadened, not constrained, to give teachers a voice on a range of important educational questions, from merit pay to curriculum. This could help improve the battered image of teachers' unions. But, more important, it could help students.

Notes

1. Terry M. Moe, *Special Interest: Teachers Unions and America's Public Schools* (Washington, DC: Brookings Institution Press, 2011), page 283, table 9–2.
2. Moe, *Special Interest*, 205.
3. Ironically, a half-century ago, Wisconsin became the first state in the nation to pass legislation allowing collective bargaining for public employees, including educators.
4. Jay P. Greene, "Unions and the Public Interest: Is Collective Bargaining for Teachers Good for Students?" *Education Next* 12, no. 1 (Winter 2012), 65.
5. Moe, *Special Interest*, 6.
6. Moe, *Special Interest*, 342.
7. Moe, *Special Interest*, 242.
8. Moe, *Special Interest*, 244.
9. United Nations General Assembly, "Universal Declaration of Human Rights," December 10, 1948, www.un.org/en/documents/udhr.
10. Ronald Reagan, Labor Day speech at Liberty State Park (Jersey City, NJ, September 1, 1980), www.reagan.utexas.edu/archives/refrence/9.1.80.html.
11. American Federation of Teachers, "States with Statutory Collective Bargaining for K–12 Teachers" (Washington, DC: American Federation of Teachers' Center for Collective Bargaining, 2011).

12. Stacey M. Childress, Denis P. Doyle, and David A. Thomas, Leading for Equity: The Pursuit of Excellence in Montgomery County Public Schools (Cambridge, MA: Harvard Education Press, 2009), 84.

13. Center for Research on Education Outcomes, *Multiple Choice: Charter School Performance in 16 States* (Stanford, CA: CREDO, 2009), http://credo.stanford.edu/reports/multiple_choice_credo.pdf.

14. Robert M. Carini, "Teacher Unions and Student Achievement," in *School Reform Proposals: The Research Evidence*, ed. Alex Molnar (Tempe, AZ: Education Policy Research Unit, 2002), http://nepc.colorado.edu/files/Chapter10-Carini-Final.pdf, page 10.17.

15. Terry M. Moe, "The Staggering Power of the Teachers' Unions," *Hoover Digest* (2011, no. 3), www.hoover.org/publications/hoover-digest/article/84076.

16. Jonathan Chait, "Learning Curve," *New Republic*, April 7, 2011.

17. Organisation for Economic Co-operation and Development, OECD Family Database, "Child Poverty," chart CO2.2.A, last updated February 28, 2011, www.oecd.org/dataoecd/52/43/41929552.pdf.

18. Organisation for Economic Co-operation and Development, OECD Family Database, "Public Spending on Education," chart PF1.2.A, last updated December 20, 2010, www.oecd.org/dataoecd/45/48/37864432.pdf.

19. David Stuit and Thomas M. Smith, "Teacher Turnover in Charter Schools" (research brief, National Center on School Choice, Peabody College of Education and Human development, Vanderbilt University, Nashville, TN, June 2010), www.vanderbilt.edu/schoolchoice/documents/briefs/brief_suit_smith_ncspe.pdf.

20. Gary Miron, testimony prepared for hearing of the House Committee on Education and the Workforce, Washington, DC, June 1, 2011, http://edworkforce.house.gov/UploadedFiles/06.01.11_miron.pdf.

21. Quote by Jonathan Alter in *Waiting for "Superman,"* directed by Davis Guggenheim, 2010.

22. Moe, *Special Interest*, 109.

23. Public Agenda, "Supporting Teacher Talent: The View from Generation Y Full Survey Results," question 40, parts c and d (data collected April 16, 2009–June 22, 2009), www.publicagenda.org/pages/supporting-teacher-talent-view-from-Generation-Y-topline.

24. Ruy Teixeira, "Public Opinion Snapshot: Public Backs Collective Bargaining Rights for State Workers," Center for American Progress, February 28, 2011, www.americanprogress.org/issues/2011/02/snapshot022811.html.

25. Hart/McInturff, NBC News/*Wall Street Journal* Survey, Study #11091, February 24–28, 2011, question 16, http://msnbcmedia.msn.com/i/MSNBC/Sections/NEWS/A_Politics/___Politics_Today_Stories_Teases/2-24-28-11.pdf.

26. Albert Shanker, "The Flagrant One-Sidedness of the Taylor Law," Where We Stand, *New York Times*, September 9, 1972, http://source.nysut.org/weblink7/DocView.aspx?id=1267.

Periodical and Internet Sources Bibliography

The following articles have been selected to supplement the diverse views presented in this chapter.

Andrew J. Coulson	"A Less Perfect Union," *American Spectator*, June 2011.
Tom DeWeese	"American Education Fails Because It Isn't Education," American Policy Center, April 11, 2011. http://americanpolicy.org/2011/04/11/american-education-fails-because-it-isnt-education-2.
Eric Hanushek	"The 'War on Teachers' Is a Myth," *Hoover Digest*, vol. 1, 2011.
Eric Hanushek and Paul E. Peterson	"Your Child Left Behind," *Hoover Digest*, vol. 2, 2011.
Susan Headden	"A Test Worth Teaching To: The Race to Fix America's Broken System of Standardized Exams," *Washington Monthly*, May–June 2012.
Jack Jennings	"Long-Term Gains in Minority Education: An Overlooked Success?," *Huffington Post*, May 8, 2011. www.huffingtonpost.com/jack-jennings/an-overlooked-success_b_857247.html.
Cheryl Miller	"The End of History in America's Classrooms," *Weekly Standard*, October 12, 2010.
Adam B. Schaeffer	"Education Cost Top Problem for Local Government," *Investor's Business Daily*, February 2, 2011.
Andrew Smarick	"The Turnaround Fallacy," *Education Next*, Winter 2010.

OPPOSING
VIEWPOINTS®
SERIES

CHAPTER 2

Are School-Choice Alternatives a Good Idea?

Chapter Preface

Proposals for allowing a choice in public education have been around as long as public schools have existed. Prior to the nationwide establishment of public schools, educational choice—including whether or not to educate at all—was simply up to parents. With the advent of public schools, however, public education is supported by all taxpayers, and all children must receive a certain level of schooling. Parents have the choice of whether or not to send their children to public school, and they have the ability to influence education policy through elected officials and being active in their local school district. Nonetheless, with federal policies such as No Child Left Behind and various state mandates on curricula, many of the facets of public school education are not open to choice by parents or students. The argument for more choice in public schooling takes a variety of forms, but what they all have in common is a desire to give more choice to parents than currently exists.

The use of school vouchers as a vehicle for choice involves giving parents a voucher equivalent to the amount of money spent per child in public school for use at a private school of their choosing. The idea of using vouchers as a way to opt out of public schools is not a new one; in the nineteenth century, Catholics asked state legislatures for state money to set up Catholic schools as an alternative to public schools. Their request was denied and most states passed constitutional provisions forbidding the use of public funds for religious schools. In 2002, however, the US Supreme Court held that public funds could be used to pay for education in religious and other private schools without violating the US Constitution's directive on separation of church and state, as long as aid went directly to parents in the form of vouchers. According to the National Conference of State Legislatures, as of October

2011, Louisiana, Indiana, Ohio, Wisconsin (Milwaukee), and the District of Columbia offer vouchers to low-income students. The use of school vouchers will likely expand around the country as a result of the Court's decision.

Similar to the option of school vouchers, but avoiding the use of direct monetary transfer, are tuition tax credits. According to the National Conference of State Legislatures, tuition tax credit programs were being used in eleven states as of September 2012. These programs allow individuals and corporations to allocate a certain portion of their owed state taxes to private, nonprofit school tuition organizations that in turn offer scholarships to students to attend one of their approved private schools, which include religious schools. Although the tuition tax credit programs do not give parents a voucher to use to attend private schools, by offering a reduction in taxes owed for participating in the program, the program essentially amounts to a monetary transfer of government funds.

In addition to these two school-choice options that allow parents some monetary support for sending children to private schools, there are also school-choice options within the public school system. Charter schools are one such option. Publicly funded and tuition free, they differ from traditional public schools by being free of some state regulations, although not from requirements on student performance. According to the National Alliance for Public Charter Schools, there were 5,275 charter schools in the 2010–2011 school year, making up more than 5 percent of all public schools.

Whether through vouchers, tax credits, or charter schools, alternatives to public schooling aimed to increase choice are not without controversy. Critics charge that diverting money and resources from the existing public school system will worsen the quality of public education, primarily benefitting families who already have the resources to send their children to private school. Additionally, there is widespread concern about the use of government funds for religious schooling, with many arguing that such a practice violates the First Amendment. Supporters of school choice claim that their right to choose how to educate their children is paramount and contend that competition is good for traditional public schools because they will be forced to improve. Nonetheless, due to widespread dissatisfaction with the quality of public school education, alternatives to public school are popular and are likely to continue to be developed and debated, as evidenced by the viewpoints in this chapter.

> *"The practical solution to America's education problems is to privatize the government school system."*

The Educational Bonanza in Privatizing Government Schools

Andrew Bernstein

In the following viewpoint, Andrew Bernstein argues that the solution to poor educational quality and the coercive nature of the current education system is to turn government schools into private schools. Bernstein claims that the free market is better equipped to offer a variety of high-quality education choices. Furthermore, he contends that a decrease in current taxes, the competitiveness of the free market, and the existence of charity will ensure the ability of all parents to send their children to school.

Andrew Bernstein is a lecturer in philosophy at the State University of New York–Purchase, and author of Capitalist Solutions: A Philosophy of American Moral Dilemmas.

As you read, consider the following questions:

1. What two policies does Bernstein claim coercively force parents to send their children to government schools?

Andrew Bernstein, "The Educational Bonanza in Privatizing Government Schools," *The Objective Standard*, vol. 5, no. 4, Winter 2010–2011, pp. 22–30. Copyright © 2011 by The Objective Standard. All rights reserved. Reproduced with permission.

2. The author claims that less than what percent of students in America attend private schools?

3. Bernstein cites the increase in parents who choose to homeschool their children in order to refute what objection to school privatization?

American education is in shambles. One in three fourth graders scores below the "basic level"—the lowest ranking deemed proficient—on the reading portion of the National Assessment of Education (NAEP) exams. Among low-income students, half score below that level. In some of America's larger cities, fewer than half the students earn a high school diploma; in Detroit, only one quarter do.[1] Roughly one million children drop out of school each year. Forty-five million Americans are marginally illiterate. Twenty-one million cannot read at all.[2]

Such statistics indicate not merely the current state of American education, but a decades-long trend in educational deterioration. Since 1983, 10 million Americans have reached twelfth grade without learning to read at the basic level. In 1986, the national test score average for eleventh graders taking the NAEP literature and history test was 54.5 percent correct on the history portion, and 51.8 percent correct on the literature portion.[3] In 1995, a nationally administered history test found that only one student in ten was grade-level proficient in the subject; the majority failed to reach a basic level.[4] In 1996, U.S. high school seniors scored near the bottom on an internationally administered math exam.[5] According to a study published in 1999, a "nationwide assessment of math skills found that 'only 14 percent of eighth graders scored at the seventh-grade level or above'"[6] and "fewer than half of twelfth-graders can do seventh-grade work in mathematics."[7] In 2000, math students in America ranked below those in Malaysia, Bulgaria, and Latvia.[8]

Why is education in America—the world's wealthiest, most-advanced nation—so abysmally bad? A central reason is the existence of America's government-run schools.

The many problems with government schools include the way they are funded, their lack of competition and economic incentive, the fact that children are forced to attend them, the schools' resultant unaccountability regardless of performance, and various other conflicts inherent in a school system based on force. Consider these in turn.

Local, state, and federal governments finance the government schools by seizing wealth from productive men, largely via property taxes, but also by means of sales and income taxes, both personal and corporate.[9] Thus the schools are funded not voluntarily, based on merit, but coercively, regardless of merit.

Indeed, on the premise that poor academic performance can be remediated primarily by increased spending, the schools receive progressively *more* money, not less, as they educationally regress. New York City in 2003, for example, in an attempt to improve the dismal academic performance of its government schools, increased spending by $7 billion, only to be dismayed by results of the 2007 NAEP exams, showing meager improvement in some areas and deterioration in others.[10]

The gradual worsening of the government schools imposes gradually heavier financial liabilities on the taxpayers who are forced to support them. The government says, in effect, "The schools are underperforming because we do not violate individual rights sufficiently; we must do so on an even wider scale."

For many families, the taxes they pay to support the government schools make it impossible for them to send their children to a private school, for they are financially unable to pay twice for education. Making matters worse, truancy laws mandate that children attend school until age sixteen. This combination of coercive policies means that many students are *forced* to attend government schools.

The current arrangement makes the government school system akin to a monopoly, in that it is impervious to competition.

By analogy, suppose the government established a state-run automobile company; legally required all adults to own a car, which they received "free" of charge; and, by means of property, sales, and income taxes, financed the government-car producer, thus making it monetarily impossible for millions of Americans to purchase a privately-manufactured automobile. Such a "business" would gain its income and "customers" by means of a rights-violating system, and it would receive the same income and "customers" regardless of whether its "customers" deemed its product satisfactory. The government-car producer would lack any and all economic incentive to excel; no matter how woeful its product, it would be kept in "business" by wealth taken coercively from taxpayers. This is what the government school system does in the realm of education.

Further, government schools create irresolvable conflicts regarding curricula, textbooks, and teacher training. In order for the government to ensure that its schools are providing government-quality education, the state must establish an agency—call it the Bureau of Education—to oversee the schools, curriculums, textbooks, and teacher training. Who controls the Bureau? In a dictatorship, the government controls it and employs the state schools to ram propaganda down the throats of its subjects. In a mixed economy, such as America's, competing interest groups vie to gain control of the Bureau, seeking to impose their preferred educational standards on the nation's youth.

Consider just a few of the conflicts arising from the current American system. Some groups want schools to teach creationism; others want them to teach evolution. Some want schools to teach the "virtues" of socialism and the "crimes" of America; others want them to teach the virtues of freedom and the unprecedented accomplishments of America. Some want schools to teach that America is a Christian country; others want them to teach that America is a secular republic. Some want schools to teach the "look-say" or "whole language" method of reading; others want schools to employ phonics.

Such conflicts follow logically from the coercive methods by which government schools are funded, populated, and operated.

By contrast, private schools entail none of these problems.

It is common knowledge that private schools are generally academically superior to government schools, and this superiority is borne out on various tests. For instance, in the area of reading, private-school fourth graders in 1994 scored nineteen points higher than their government school counterparts on the NAEP exam.[11] Likewise, in the field of math, also during the 1990s, the disparity between private school and government school achievement, on average, over the course of high school, was equivalent to 3.2 years of learning.[12] More recently, in 2008, educational researcher Andrew Coulson reported on a comprehensive study—analyzing twenty-five years of educational research from eighteen nations—that compared government schools to private schools. The analysis demonstrated not merely the academic superiority of private education, but, more revealingly, that "the private sector's margin of superiority is greatest when looking at the least regulated, most market-like private schools."[13]

One school that demonstrated both the superiority of the private model and the problems for private schools posed by government schools was Westside Preparatory School in Chicago, founded in 1975 by Marva Collins. Collins was a schoolteacher in Chicago who, frustrated by the bureaucratic restrictions of the government schools, resigned and opened

Westside Prep. She took in many low-income and minority children deemed incorrigibly uneducable by the same government schools she had fled and transformed them into consummate students. She jettisoned the look-say and whole-language methods of teaching reading used in the government schools, taught phonics instead, and made reading a vital part of every aspect of her curriculum, including mathematics. She did not organize classes based exclusively on age, but let students progress as rapidly as they were able, and used advanced students to assist in the teaching of novices. Both she and her school became justly famous for the academic excellence achieved by their students.[14] Unfortunately, due to insufficient enrollment and funding, Westside Prep closed in 2008 while government schools in Chicago continued to receive both students and funding by means of coercion.

Countless comparisons of private schools to government schools reveal that the former generally outperform the latter. The question is: Why?

The main reason for private school superiority is that such schools are *immune* to the problems that inescapably plague government schools.

A private school cannot force customers to purchase its product, nor can it compel anyone to finance its existence, nor can it regulate or curtail the activities of its competitors. Because private schools are legally forbidden to use force, their existence and programs entail no violation of rights. Having to earn their customers and money, private schools possess strong economic incentive to provide excellent educational services. If they want to stay in business and flourish, they must make money by satisfying the educational requirements of students and their families; if they fail to do so, they face bankruptcy. (Even nonprofit private schools must compete for students and funding. If they fail to deliver a satisfactory educational product, families send their children to a competitor that does. And if they fail to succeed in their stated mission, their philanthropic financiers will find other venues for their philanthropy.)

Further, private schools pose no irresolvable problems of curriculum, textbooks, or teaching methods. The *owners* of private schools decide what subjects will be taught, the methods by which they will be taught, and the price at which they will offer their services. Parents voluntarily purchase the service for their children (or not) and continue to purchase it only if satisfied with the service and its price.

If a private school chooses to teach the theory of evolution in its biology curriculum, it is free to do so, and potential customers are free to decide whether they want that for their children. If another private school chooses to teach creationism, it is free to do so, and potential customers are free to decide whether they want *that* for their children. If a private school chooses to focus on the three Rs to the exclusion of painting, music, or drama, it is free to do so, and potential customers are free to patronize the school or not. If another private school chooses to focus on the arts, or to focus on trade skills, or to offer any variety of subjects, it is free to do so, and potential customers are free to do business there or not.

The philosophy of education is a complex and controversial issue, and people's needs and values can differ in countless ways. In a system of private schools, everyone is free to decide what he will do with his money and where he will educate his child; no one is forced to finance schools he deems unworthy or to patronize ideas he deems false or immoral.

In short, private schools do not violate rights; thus, they are free of the myriad problems that accompany rights violations. In other words, private schools are not only moral but also—and consequently—*practical.*

History demonstrates this as fully as do current educational practices.

Prior to the mid-19th century, government schools did not exist in America. All schools were private, and education was widespread and outstanding. For example, in the Middle Atlantic colonies during the pre-Revolutionary period, professional educators established numerous schools to satisfy the demand for education.[15] Philadelphia, for instance, boasted schools for every subject and interest. Between 1740 and 1776, 125 private schoolmasters advertised their services in Philadelphia newspapers—this in a city whose population was miniscule relative to today. Professional educators provided mentoring services in English, contemporary foreign languages, science, and a wide variety of other topics.[16] Children who grew to be such brilliant scientists, writers, and statesmen as Benjamin Franklin, Thomas Jefferson, and George Washington received their education at home or in private schools.

(As to higher education, by the late-18th century six private colleges operated in the colonies: Yale, the College of New Jersey [Princeton], the College of Philadelphia [Penn], Dartmouth, Queen's [Rutgers], and Rhode Island College [Brown].)[17]

Predictably, the educational results of such a free educational market were superb. The literacy levels of Revolutionary America were remarkably high. For example, Thomas Paine's book, *Common Sense*, written in plain style but enunciating sophisticated political principles, sold 120,000 copies during the colonial period to a free population of 2.4 million (akin to selling 10 million copies today).[18] The essays of *The Federalist*, written by Hamilton, Madison, and Jay in support of a Constitution for the nascent republic, were largely newspaper editorials written for and read by the common man.

Sales of American books and educational materials in the early- and mid-19th century likewise indicate a high national literacy rate. Between 1818 and 1823, while the U.S. population was under 20 million, Walter Scott's novels sold 5 million copies (the equivalent of selling 60 million copies today).

Early in the 19th century, *The Last of the Mohicans* by James Fenimore Cooper likewise sold millions of copies.[19] The *McGuffey's Readers*, first published in 1836, routinely used such terms as "heath" and "benighted" in third-grade texts. They asked such questions as "What is this species of composition called?" and gave such assignments as "Relate the facts of this dialogue." The fourth-grade reader included selections from Hawthorne, and the fifth-grade text, readings from Shakespeare. "These were not the textbooks of the elite but of the masses," explains Thomas Sowell. "[F]rom 1836 to 1920, *McGuffey's Readers* were so widely used that they sold more than 122 million copies."[20]

Given the high quality of education in early America, it is no surprise that two renowned French visitors observed and reported on the phenomenon. In an 1800 book Vice President Thomas Jefferson commissioned, titled *National Education in the United States of America*, Pierre Du Pont de Nemours reported that Americans received an education far superior to that of other peoples. "Most young Americans," he wrote, "can read, write, and cipher. Not more than four in a thousand are unable to write legibly."[21] Several decades later, Alexis de Tocqueville wrote in *Democracy in America* that Americans were the most educated people of history.[22]

Private schools in America have provided and continue to provide high-quality education.

Unfortunately, private schools today constitute less than 11 percent of America's educational system. According to the National Center for Educational Statistics, in school year 2009–2010, nearly 49.8 million students attended government schools, while 5.8 million were enrolled in private schools.[23] Because of the numerous coercive laws earlier discussed, almost 90 percent of American children are *compelled* to attend educationally crippling government schools. This is not merely a tragedy. It is a man-made tragedy; indeed, an atrocity.

What is the solution?

One key political solution to the abysmal state of education in America is to privatize the government schools. For an indication of what would happen to education in America if the government schools were privatized, consider the industries that are either fully or essentially private. Examine the quality, availability, and prices of automobiles, cell phones, CDs, MP3 players, jeans, breakfast cereals, and pain relievers. Consider the quality, availability, and prices of services such as hair styling, car repair, plumbing, and dentistry. If we focus on any one of these, we can see that the private nature of the businesses involved is what drives quality up, prices down, and makes such a diverse array of goods and services available to millions.

For instance, when was the last time anyone complained about a shortage of high-quality, low-priced cell phones? Observe that there are countless varieties of cell phones, optional features, and calling plans. Cellular service producers competing for business provide customers with sparkling new, high-tech phones *free of charge* upon contracting to purchase their service. Just over a century ago, people had no telephone service. Now they receive a personal, portable phone—a technological marvel—for free. Why are cell phones and calling plans so inexpensive, technologically advanced, and abundant? The answer is that the industry is relatively free of government interference. Producers of goods and services in a free market know that if they provide quality products for reasonable prices they will make money and that if they do not they will go out of business.

The economic bottom line is that if a producible good or service is in demand in a free market, profit-seeking businessmen will endeavor to supply it at affordable prices. Education is no exception.

In a fully privatized, free market of education, profit-seeking businessmen would provide quality educational services at prices affordable to millions. And because they would have to meet consumer demand in order to thrive, business-men would provide a sweeping diversity of services matching actual student needs. For example, observing that many people value the full academic curriculum and want their children to learn the classic three Rs of reading, writing, and arithmetic, entrepreneurial educators would provide such a service effectively and affordably. Likewise, observing that many of these same people want their children later to advance to science, mathematics, literature, and history, educators would provide these services as well, because they could make money doing so.

The same is true of vocational training. Some families demand only the basics of academics, and then want their children to branch out into one of many vocational fields—whether business, farming, baking, construction work, or countless other productive fields. In a free market, profit-seeking educators would supply such services as efficiently and inexpensively as possible—lest competitors provide a better value and put them out of business.

This truth applies also to the field of special education. Some individuals need specialized instruction. For example, some are gifted in specific ways—intellectually, musically, athletically—and require highly focused, advanced training. Others suffer from debilitating psychological or physiological ailments. Some are sadly afflicted with varying degrees of mental retardation. In a free market, where there is a demand for various forms of special education, profit-seeking businessmen will compete to supply them.

All the evidence culled from the current state of education, from history, and from the logic of economics points without exception to a single conclusion: Private schools competing for students and profits in free (or freer) markets produce quality, affordable educational services to satisfy customer demand.

Politically speaking, the practical solution to America's education problems is to privatize the government school system—to convert the government schools into private schools. And the reason this is the practical solution is that it is the *moral* solution. A fully private school system would recognize and respect the rights of everyone involved. It would leave educators and customers fully free to produce and purchase educational products and services in accordance with their own needs and preferences. . . .

Before we turn to *how* the government school system should be privatized, let us address a couple of common objections to the goal of privatization.

One objection is that some parents do not value their children's education enough to pay for it. To the extent that there are such parents, this is hardly a reason to violate the rights of all Americans and destroy the possibility of a good education for millions of other children. People who have children and do not care enough to educate them should be socially ostracized and, when appropriate, prosecuted for parental neglect. But they should not be held up as a reason to violate Americans' rights and keep American education in the sewer.

The fact is that the overwhelming preponderance of parents value their children's education *enormously* and, when free to choose how they would spend their money, would procure that value just as they do food, clothing, shelter, and medical care. Observe in this regard the current trend toward home schooling in America. An increasing number of parents, now more than a million, value their children's education so much and are so dissatisfied with government schools that they have chosen to home school their children—despite the fact that they are still forced to finance the government schools they do not use. (Not surprisingly, the educational results achieved by home schoolers are generally outstanding. For example, by eighth grade most home-schooled children test four grade levels above the national average.)[24]

If parents choose not to provide their children with a proper education, that is their right—and the children will, for a time, suffer the consequences of their parents' irrationality. But children are not mindless replicates of their parents; as they grow into adulthood they can and often do make fundamentally different choices. For example, the children of religious parents sometimes choose secularism; the offspring of bigoted parents often choose individualism; and the children of alcoholic or drug-addicted parents often choose clean living. Human beings possess free will, and, as numerous parents ruefully learn, their children frequently do not passively accept their families' values.

Even in today's government-thwarted education market, many centers of adult education prosper. A fully free market in education would enable educational entrepreneurs to expand this market immensely. Competition among private schools and tutors providing both academic and vocational training for the adult market would increase; prices would drop; options would abound. In such a marketplace, the few children whose backward parents had neglected to educate them could seek education on their own in their early years of adulthood, then move on and live lives of greater wisdom and superior career opportunities.

Finally, it is important to emphasize that there is no right to an education—just as there is no right to food, shelter, or medical care. A right involves the freedom to act on one's best judgment and to pursue the values of one's choice. It does not involve access to a good or service at someone else's expense. If a person (or a citizenry) is forced to provide others with education (or anything else), then his rights are violated and he becomes, to that extent, a slave of those he involuntarily serves. A free market in education would both obviate such manifest immorality and provide immensely better options in all educational fields.

Another objection to a fully privatized educational system is that if taxpayers were not coerced to finance government schools, some families would be unable to afford quality education. The first thing to note in answer to this objection is that the coercively funded and operated government schools are precisely what make it impossible for customers to receive quality education. Another important point is that with the government monolith slain, the property, income, and sales taxes that had been levied to sustain it could and should be repealed. With their tax burden substantially diminished, families would retain more of their income and be fully free to spend it on their children's education. Yet another point is that in a full private market for education, competition among private schools, teachers, and tutors would increase dramatically. This inevitably would drive prices down, making education increasingly affordable.

As for those families that somehow in a free market for education still could not afford to pay for any education for their children, observe that even today many private schools offer scholarships to worthy students who cannot meet the tuition.[25] In a fully free market for education, such scholarships would increase and abound. Private schools are highly competitive with one another, and they all seek to showcase the value and superiority of their product. Consequently, it is in their rational self-interest to attract students who will make them shine. Scholarships are a crucial means of doing so.

It is also worth noting that voluntary charity flourishes in America even when we are taxed at today's obscene rates. According to Giving USA Foundation's annual report on philanthropy, "Charitable giving in the United States exceeded $300 billion for the second year in a row in 2008," and "Education organizations received an estimated $40.94 billion, or 13 percent of the total."[26] So long as the government does not prohibit educational charities, Americans will contribute to such charities.

In short, in a fully private market for education, the few families unable to afford quality education would find no shortage of scholarships and/or charities available to assist them. Objections to privatizing the government schools simply do not hold water.

Now let us turn to the question of how government schools could be privatized.

There are, no doubt, several viable means by which this could be done, but one straightforward way is simply by auctioning off schools and their corresponding properties to the highest bidders. Sold schools would either continue under private ownership, or the properties would be used for noneducational purposes. If the schools became private schools, competition in a free market would ensure a drive toward improved education and decreased prices. If some of the properties were deployed for noneducational purposes, the resultant increase in demand for education in that area would motivate profit-seeking educational entrepreneurs to meet the demand with other venues. Either way, the market would soon teem with private schools, teachers, and tutors competing to supply the educational service demanded by millions of families whose only earlier alternative was the abysmally bad government school system.

Such a transition would necessarily take some time, and the government would have to provide fair notice and appropriate grace periods to enable government-dependent families to adjust to the free market. For instance, the government could enact a law declaring that, effective immediately, the government would begin auctioning off school properties, with transference of ownership to occur at the end of a five-year grace period. This would enable all teachers, tutors, and educational entrepreneurs to ramp up their businesses. And it would give all parents substantial time to assume full responsibility for the education of their children.

The enactment of such a policy would be followed by an explosion of private schools and tutoring services, some large-scale, others small; some in private homes (as Marva Collins began), some in multistory buildings; some religious, some secular; some profit-driven, some not. The teeming diversity of schools and the high level of educational results would soon rival those of America in the centuries before the imposition of government schooling.

We who recognize the vital nature of education to the lives of individuals and to the health of a society must demand the privatization of government-run schools and work toward the establishment of a fully private market in education. The time to advocate this change is now.

Endnotes

1. Dan Lips, "Still a Nation at Risk," www.heritage.org/Research/Commentary2008/05/Still A Nation at Risk.
2. "Reading, Literacy & Education Statistics," www.readfaster.com/education.asp.
3. Diane Ravitch and Chester Finn, *What Do Our 17 Year Olds Know?: A Report of the First National Assessment of History and Literature* (New York: Harper & Row, 1987), pp. 1, 43, 120; Andrew Coulson, *Market Education: The Unknown History* (New Brunswick, NJ: Transaction Publishers, 1999), pp. 188–89.
4. Coulson, *Market Education*, pp. 8–10.
5. C. Bradley Thompson, "Cognitive Math Abuse in Our Classrooms," www.aynrand.org/site/News2?page=NewsArticle&id=5410.
6. Coulson, *Market Education*, p. 9.
7. Coulson, *Market Education*, p. 15.
8. Thompson, "Cognitive Math Abuse."
9. "Trends in Educational Funding—Public Schools: Where Does The Money Come From?," http://social.jrank.org/pages/965/Trends-in-Educational-Funding-Public-Schools-Where-Does-Money-Come-From.html.

10. Sol Stern, "In School Reform, Billions of Dollars But Not Much Bang," www.manhattaninstitute.org/html/miarticle .htm?id=4167.

11. Coulson, *Market Education*, pp. 279–86.

12. Coulson, *Market Education*, p. 280.

13. "Markets of Competing Private Schools Outperform Public School, Study Based on 25 Years of Educational Data Effectively Settles the Debate," Cato Institute news release, September 10, 2008, www.cato.org/pressroom.php?display= news&id=157. Coulson's full report, "Markets vs. Monopolies in Education: A Global Review of the Evidence," is available here: http://www.cato.org/pubs/pas/pa620.pdf.

14. Marva Collins and Civia Tamarkin, *Marva Collins' Way* (New York: Putnam, 1990), pp. 126–37.

15. Hans Sennholz, ed., *Public Education and Indoctrination* (Irvington-on-Hudson, NY: Foundation for Economic Education, 1993), p. 38.

16. Sennholz, *Public Education*, pp. 22–23, 26, 38–39, 44.

17. Sennholz, *Public Education*, p. 23. Harvard was founded by the Great and General Court of the Massachusetts Bay Colony and named for its first donor, John Harvard. The College of William & Mary and King's College (Columbia University) were founded by royal charter.

18. Sheldon Richman, *Separating School and State* (Fairfax, VA: The Future of Freedom Foundation, 1995), p. 38.

19. Richman, *Separating School and State*, p. 38.

20. Thomas Sowell, *Inside American Education: The Decline, the Deception, the Dogmas* (New York: The Free Press, 1993), p. 7.

21. Pierre Du Pont de Nemours, *National Education in the United States of America*, translated from the second French edition of 1812 and with an introduction by B. G. Du Pont (Newark, DE: University of Delaware Press, 1923), pp. 3–4; quoted in Sennholz, *Public Education*, pp. 23–24.

22. Sennholz, *Public Education*, p. 44; John Taylor Gatto, "Our Prussian School System," *Cato Policy Report*, March/April 1993, p. 1.
23. National Center for Educational Statistics, U.S. Department of Education, Fast Facts, http://nces.ed.gov/fastfacts/display.asp?id=372.
24. Isabel Lyman, *The Homeschooling Revolution* (Amherst, MA: Bench Press International, 2000), pp. 59–69.
25. Melissa Kelly, "Teaching at Private vs. Public Schools," http://712educators.about.com/od/jobopenings/a/private-public.htm.
26. "U.S. Charitable Giving Estimated to Be $307.65 Billion in 2008," Giving USA Foundation, http://www.philanthropy.iupui.edu/News/2009/docs/GivingReaches300billion_06102009.pdf.

> "The value of a strong public school system could not be more obvious than it is now, as we face the prospect of losing it altogether."

The Republican War on Education

Ruth Conniff

In the following viewpoint, Ruth Conniff argues that the battle over Wisconsin's Senate Bill 22 (since defeated) is evidence of a frightening war on public education that threatens to privatize schools. Conniff contends that the proposal to replace public schools with charter schools—both physical and virtual (online)—is opposed by large numbers of the public and is undemocratic. Conniff claims the support for privatization comes from big business and politicians who are beholden to lobbyists, not from teachers and others who care about education.

Ruth Conniff is the political editor of the Progressive, *a monthly magazine with a liberal perspective.*

As you read, consider the following questions:

1. What is the single largest budget item for each of the fifty states, according to Conniff?

Ruth Conniff, "The Republican War on Education," *Progressive*, vol. 75, no. 5, May 2011.

2. The author cites a study by Stanford University showing that what percentage of charter schools performed better and what percentage performed worse than public schools?

3. Conniff cites what examples of interaction between teacher and students, recounted by a Wisconsin teacher, that are not available through a virtual education?

The public outpouring was incredible. People flooded into the capitol building in Madison, Wisconsin, from the urban neighborhoods of Milwaukee and from tiny towns in the northern and western corners of the state. They came to oppose Republican plans that would wipe out rural school districts, drain resources from city schools, and dismantle an entire statewide system of public education.

They packed a hearing room and two overflow rooms, and waited all day to speak. Hour after hour, teachers, parents, and citizens gave impassioned, often tearful testimony. Jon Sheller, a former member of the Montello school board, and his daughter, social studies teacher Yedda Ligocki, talked about their little town, with 750 schoolchildren. "As in most small school districts," Sheller said, the school "is the heart of the community."

"The athletics, the musicals, other school activities are the life of Montello," added Ligocki.

Governor Scott Walker's unprecedented $900 million cut to school funding, coupled with a scheme [Senate Bill (S.B.) 22] to create a state-run system of charter schools, will kill off both the school and the town, they said. Under S.B. 22, the bill they came to oppose, students and funds that used to go to schools like Montello's will be siphoned off to virtual charter schools run by a state board of political appointees.

"There will be no turning back," Sheller said. "Small schools and their communities will wither and die—and for what? A political maneuver to allow privatization of public education at the expense of Wisconsin's history as a leader in student achievement. This is giving away our future."

Wisconsin is on the leading edge of a national assault on public education. Walker made a big name for himself with his explosive move to bust public employee unions and take away teachers' bargaining rights. Now comes the next phase.

"We've been hearing about this for years now," says Democratic state representative Sondy Pope-Roberts. "I see Wisconsin as the first domino in a line. As this falls, I see other states hoping to achieve our quote-unquote success . . . by crushing unions and taking public schools private."

Wisconsin has long had a strong public school system. But the conservative Bradley Foundation in Milwaukee has also been a national incubator for vouchers and other school privatization efforts.

"We started by being the first state to have a voucher school, in Milwaukee," Pope-Roberts says. "Now we will be the first state to . . . basically create charter school districts."

Instead of being approved by local school boards, under S.B. 22 these charters would be overseen by a nine-member board appointed by the governor and leaders of the legislature.

The bill would encourage the rapid expansion of virtual charters, which would receive the same per-pupil tax dollars as bricks-and-mortar schools, and could enroll students all over the state.

Walker's other proposals include lifting the income cap for vouchers, so wealthy families could receive public funds to send their kids to private schools.

The war on public schools is part of the conservative dream to "get government down to the size where you can drown it in the bathtub," as conservative guru Grover Norquist so memorably put it.

K–12 education is the single largest budget item for each of the 50 states. So it stands to reason that privatizing education is the largest front in the conservative war on government.

Hence the jarring attacks on teachers by Walker and his political allies in Ohio, Michigan, Indiana, and Pennsylvania.

But it turns out that drowning students and teachers in the bathtub isn't all that popular with the public.

"I'm seeing this kernel of negativity and meanness in this bill," said Milwaukee resident Lorraine Jacobs in her testimony before the senate education committee in Madison.

As Lisa Scofield, a parent in Spring Green who teaches in the River Valley School District, put it, "This is not about education. It's about money and control, and you are taking it away. How can you even pretend to strengthen education as you dismantle our state's largest democratic institution?"

On the statewide expansion of charter schools, 120 people testified. Of these, only fifteen were in favor, and twelve of those fifteen were people with a direct interest in charter schools.

Republican senator Alberta Darling, the supposed author of the bill, introduced it flanked by its real authors—state and national charter school organizations. "These gentlemen represent a massive network," she declared.

Todd Ziebarth of the National Alliance for Public Charter Schools testified that Wisconsin "fails to provide autonomy" to charters. David Hansen of the National Association of Charter School Authorizers said S.B. 22 would make Wisconsin a better "policy environment," allowing more charters to open. If they failed, his organization could simply close them down.

This idea that it's no big deal to close down schools is perhaps the biggest disconnect between business-minded school "reformers" and the parents and teachers who came out to plead with their legislators not to destroy the public school system.

"I don't want my children's school in someone's portfolio," said Scofield, objecting to the business lingo used by the bill's proponents. "I want it in my community, with local control."

"I just wonder who is benefitting from this," she added. "Because it's not my kids."

"Charter schools are public schools," the charter advocates repeatedly intoned. John Gee, executive director of the Wisconsin Charter Schools Association, went even further, saying kids who can't afford private education need a way out of failing schools: "Ultimately, this is a social justice issue," he said, to a chorus of groans.

Gee was referring to historic racial divisions over school choice. When the Bradley Foundation made private-school vouchers into a national crusade, it pushed African American parents in Milwaukee out front on the issue. After all, who wants to argue with low-income, minority parents that their kids should be trapped in lousy schools?

The Madison Urban League's Kaleem Caire testified that S.B. 22 would make it easier for him to open a charter school for African American boys who are not well served by the public schools.

But overall, Walker's education proposals face opposition from both public school advocates and black leaders like Milwaukee's state senator Lena Taylor, who acknowledges that school choice is a tough issue.

"What we've done with this budget is to set up a secondary system of education with its own rules," says Democratic state representative Fred Clark.

If Wisconsin Republicans succeed in setting up their new statewide system of charter schools, Madison school board member Marjorie Passman testified, "those not chosen by lottery will return to the dying embers of our public school system."

"Add vouchers to the picture," Passman said, "and you'll actually have the poor paying for the rich to attend school."

The Rush to Privatize Education

From Idaho to Indiana to Florida, recently passed laws will radically reshape the face of education in America, shifting the responsibility of teaching generations of Americans to online education businesses, many of which have poor or nonexistent track records. The rush to privatize education will also turn tens of thousands of students into guinea pigs in a national experiment in virtual learning—a relatively new idea that allows for-profit companies to administer public schools completely online, with no brick-and-mortar classrooms or traditional teachers.

Lee Fang, Nation, *December 5, 2011.*

That, in a nutshell, is the vision of Walker and the coalition of interest groups that helped draft his education policies.

There is nothing remotely democratic about it. In fact, it is the brainchild of a network of national privatization think tanks and lobby groups. Just listen to the buzzwords that pop up over and over as Republican governors and legislators across the country attack teachers' unions, cut education budgets, and privatize schools.

Governor Walker used the word "tools" with Tourette's-like frequency during a press conference on his education program.

"We're giving our schools and local governments the tools they need" to make needed reform, he said, which amounts to "a net benefit to school districts."

If districts seize the "tools" and drive a hard bargain with teachers, they can save a lot of money, the governor asserted.

There is something funny about that word "tools."

It popped up again in Ohio, when Governor John Kasich announced a massive 16.4 percent cut to the state's education system. A press release from a think tank called Ohio Education Matters, which helped draft Kasich's plan, praised the governor's education effort, saying it "provides the right tools to help schools meet lower spending levels."

Those "tools" include cutting teacher benefits and "expanding opportunities for digital education." Digital education turns out to be the business of the group's parent organization, KnowledgeWorks, which markets a "portfolio of innovative approaches" to schools in seventeen states.

On the cover of the January 2011 issue of the pro-business American Legislative Exchange Council's magazine, *Inside ALEC*, there is a large photo of a toolbox and the headline "State Budget Reform Toolkit." ALEC drafts boilerplate legislation and pushes a pro-privatization agenda to state legislators around the country.

While there are good charter schools that work with local districts, independent charters are part of the "toolkit" of privatization and budget cutting around the nation. Robert Bobb, emergency manager of the Detroit Public Schools, has proposed a massive conversion of the city's schools to charters to deal with budget cuts. The rationale: Replacing all of Detroit's teachers with non-union personnel would save the district money.

Nor are charters better. In Philadelphia, a 2010 federal investigation turned up evidence of rampant fraud and mismanagement in the city's charters. The only comprehensive, national study of charters, by Stanford University, found that only 17 percent outperformed public schools, 37 percent did significantly worse, and the remaining 46 percent were no better. Likewise, Milwaukee voucher students perform worse in state tests than their public school peers. But liquidating state education funds, especially if you don't have to pay union wages or benefits, especially if you don't even have to maintain a physical building, means big money.

On education, money is lined up against students, teachers, and local communities—from the inner city to little farm towns.

It is telling that in Wisconsin, just as the Republicans won both houses of the legislature and moved into leadership positions, top staffers left state government altogether to take new jobs—as school privatization lobbyists. "The voucher groups are the heavies now," says Democratic state representative Mark Pocan. "Bankers and realtors have become the B team."

James Bender, former chief of staff for now-majority leader Jeff Fitzgerald, is currently a lobbyist for School Choice Wisconsin.

Brian Pleva, who ran the powerful Republican Assembly Campaign Committee, joined indicted former assembly speaker Scott Jensen at the Washington, D.C.–based American Federation for Children, a spinoff of the Michigan-based group All Children Matter, which has poured millions into phony issue ads in state legislative races. All Children Matter was founded by Michigan billionaires Dick and Betsy DeVos.

American Federation for Children spent $820,000 in the last election cycle in Wisconsin—almost as much as the $1 million spent by the state's most powerful coalition of business groups, Wisconsin Manufacturers and Commerce.

School choice groups form, dissolve, and then spring up again with new, patriotic-sounding names in each election cycle, says Mike McCabe, executive director of the watchdog group Wisconsin Democracy Campaign. That way they can remain nonprofits, instead of 527s [election campaign groups organized under Section 527 of the Internal Revenue Code], and they don't have to disclose their donors.

So there you have it: money and political power bearing down on public school teachers and kids with all the force of a mighty, well-financed, nationally organized lobby.

Patricia Schmidt, a white-haired elementary school music teacher from Republican education committee chair Senator Luther Olsen's district, told the committee "Wautoma schools are bracing for the worst."

Because of budget cuts, Schmidt said, she is driving to nearby Redgranite and teaching 100 extra students. "Our music program is very strong, and many of our students would drop out if they couldn't sing in the choir or play in the band, because they're not doing so well in their other classes," she said. Virtual schools would never fill the gap if her school closed, she added. She pleaded with the senators on the committee to come see the students and teachers for themselves.

Weirdly, bill sponsor Darling, who seemed distracted for much of the hearing, woke up from her reverie and thanked the music teacher for doing such a good job with the kids.

Few politicians want to appear in public being mean to white-haired music teachers.

But at the hearing, Republican state legislators had to sit and listen to their constituents tell them that they are going down in history as the people who killed their hometowns.

It's a pretty damn dramatic problem for Darling, Olsen, and others who are facing energized recall campaigns, thanks to Walker's scorched-earth program.

Drowning government in the bathtub is all well and good until you're the one who has to do the wet work.

So we got the bizarre scene in the hearing room: platitudes from politicians about "reforming" education in order to "help children," and citizens reacting with shock to the reality of brutal budget cuts and a vicious, predatory privatization scheme.

While Darling fiddled with her cell phone and whispered to her staff, Montello's Ligocki tried to describe what is important about local schools and their real, flesh-and-blood teachers.

She talked about her relationship with her high school English teacher and mentor, Miss Maasz.

When Maasz was about to lose her battle with cancer, Ligocki went to see her. "I asked her to tell me everything I needed to know about being a teacher in the few minutes we had to talk," Ligocki said. "She summarized decades of teaching experience with this sentence: 'When you walk into that classroom, your number one job is to love your students, and the ones who are the hardest to love are the ones who need it the most.' That sentence did more to prepare me for teaching than I could have imagined."

Ligocki went on to describe working in a school where half the kids qualify for free or reduced lunch, in an area plagued by poverty and alcoholism. "Many of our students' parents can't or don't give them the care they need," Ligocki said. "I don't just teach my kids, I love them. I raise them."

She talked about keeping extra food on hand for kids who are hungry. She told how she intervened when she saw that they were being abused. She explained how she earns their trust so they are willing to make themselves vulnerable and to try their hardest to learn.

Recently, during a training in online teaching, Ligocki said she asked her instructor, a virtual school teacher, about his relationships with students. "He said it was mostly limited to e-mails and comments on discussion boards."

The same day, she said, she went to a funeral for a beloved local math teacher, Andy Polk, a young husband and father who was killed in a tractor accident.

Students and teachers stood in the rain for two hours waiting to get inside the school for the visitation. "Students made huge displays with poems, pictures, and their favorite Mr. Polk sayings," she said.

"The shortcomings of a virtual education could not have been more obvious that day."

And the value of a strong public school system could not be more obvious than it is now, as we face the prospect of losing it altogether.

> *"The choice of increasing student outcomes by moving to vouchers is becoming more and more of a no-brainer."*

School Vouchers Are a Good Alternative to Public Schools

Gary Jason

In the following viewpoint, Gary Jason argues that allowing parents to use vouchers to pay for their children to attend the school of their choice is the solution to the problems present in the American public education system. Jason claims that recent research shows that voucher schools have better outcomes than public schools with respect to student performance, improving competition, improving graduation rates, and decreasing school violence.

Gary Jason is an adjunct philosophy professor at California State University–Fullerton and a senior editor of Liberty, *a libertarian journal.*

As you read, consider the following questions:

1. According to the author, per capita education spending has increased by what factor over the last quarter of a century?

2. Jason cites a study showing that voucher competition led to gains in reading performance in what two groups of public school students?

3. The author contends that a study of the Milwaukee voucher program shows that among voucher students, the graduation rate was how much higher?

The failure of the American K–12 public school system has been obvious for decades. Some of us fossils can recall the public uproar that accompanied the release of the report "A Nation at Risk" back in 1987, documenting the mediocre at best, disastrously bad at worst performance of the nation's public schools.[1]

A Solution to the Education Problem

The public school special interest groups (the PSSIGs)—that is, public school administrators, education department professors, "labor studies" professors, textbook publishers, and most notoriously teachers unions and their members—managed to turn the outrage into support for jacking up spending.

Over the last quarter-century, we have nearly doubled our national per capita spending—we now outspend per capita for K–12 education every other nation on Earth but one. But our national student scores have remained flat, while internationally, we have dropped in ranking among developed nations from 14th during the 1970s down to 24th place [in 2011].

Fabulous news, however: our students still outscore the other kids of the world on—self-esteem!

Milton Friedman, the Nobel Prize–winning economist and public intellectual, devised an elegantly simple but profound solution to the problem: vouchers. Under the voucher concept, the money we the taxpayers give—yes, it is our money,

---

1. *A Nation at Risk* was the 1983 report of President Ronald Reagan's National Commission on Excellence in Education that claimed America's schools were failing and called for education reforms to boost student achievement.

not the PSSIGSs'—to support public education is divided equally and goes directly to the children (through their parents), as opposed to being funneled through a giant rent-seeking machine. A brilliant, cut-to-the-chase concept: empower the users of a government-promoted service to pick the venue that best suits them, as opposed to what suits the providers of the service.

This fits well with Kantian [after eighteenth-century German philosopher Immanuel Kant] ethics: it respects the dignity of autonomous individuals by letting them choose the path that leads to their greatest self-fulfillment.

Voucher Students' Performance

Recent studies confirm consequentially what reasoning suggests logically. For example, a meta-study [a study of many studies] by the superb social scientist, Greg Forster, reviews the literature on voucher programs, and it is quite positive.

He notes that of the ten "gold standard" studies of vouchers—that is, studies that look at the performance of kids who won the lottery to go to voucher schools versus those who entered the lottery but lost (so had to attend public schools instead—nine show statistically significant gains in academic performance, and the one exception did show gains, just not at the level of statistical significance. By comparing students who got the vouchers with those who tried but didn't get them, these studies effectively rule out other possible explanations for the academic gains, such as parental or student ambition.

Forster also reports that of the 19 empirical studies of the impact voucher schools have on the surrounding public schools, 18 confirm what one would expect *a priori* [without having to see evidence], viz. [namely], that competition from the voucher schools would force the public ones to improve their services. The remaining study shows no impact—but no harm, either.

Reasons for School Vouchers

Even if vouchers did not improve test scores for participants and public schools, there would still be other reasons to implement them. Vouchers put students into schools that graduate more students, earn significantly greater satisfaction from parents, provide better services for disabled students, improve racial integration and students' civic values, save the public money, and so forth.

There are also other reasons one might support vouchers independent of their impact on test scores. Perhaps the most important argument is that they return control of education to parents, where it had rested for much of our nation's history. The seizure of power over education by a government monopoly and attendant interest groups (especially unions) has had far-reaching implications for our nation. The American founders would have viewed it as incompatible with a free and democratic society, as well as a realistic understanding of the natural formation of the human person in the family.

However, when all these issues have been considered, the empirical question of how vouchers impact student test scores remains—and it remains important. Vouchers do, in fact, improve test scores for both participants and public schools. The benefits of competition in education are clearly established by the evidence. The only remaining question is whether the evidence will be permitted to shape public debate on the question of vouchers.

Greg Forster, Foundation for Education Choice, March 2011.

The Impact of Public Schools

Another study by Matthew Carr provides yet more evidence of the validity of the voucher concept.

Carr researched the Ohio voucher program, called the Educational Choice Scholarship Program ("EdChoice") and passed by the legislature there in 2005. EdChoice provides vouchers to a small number of public school students. EdChoice was fiercely opposed by Ohio's PSSIGs then, and current Republican Governor [John] Kasich is facing even fiercer PSSIG resistance now as he struggles to quadruple the number of vouchers available to students in failing public schools.

Carr's study focuses on the crucial claim that voucher schools make public schools improve their quality of service through the force of competition (what he terms "the voucher threat"). Carr found that the public schools facing the voucher threat showed statistically significant gains in reading compared with those who didn't.

Interestingly, the gains are most concentrated in the "tails of the Bell-shaped curve"—that is, the most advanced and least advanced students. As he puts it, this suggests that the public schools facing voucher competition put their focus on improving their services to the two groups they view as most likely to flee to private schools.

Neither Forster nor Carr reviews the studies done in other countries—such as Denmark; New Zealand; Sweden; and Quebec, Canada—that have national voucher programs. But those studies show that vouchers work to improve student outcomes, and that teachers like the results just as the parents do.

Other Benefits of School Vouchers

Even more exciting is the recent work by researchers investigating the effects of voucher programs on such non-academic but still vitally important phenomena as graduation rates and rates of campus violence. Here the results are even more dramatic.

The 2010 study of the D.C. voucher program done by the U.S. Department of Education—a study that President [Barack] Obama shamefully suppressed while he killed the

D.C. voucher system (even as he was finding the best private school for his own privileged children)—shows that the students who went to voucher schools had a 21% higher graduation rate than students who applied for vouchers but lost the lottery (91% versus 70%).

A similar study of the Milwaukee voucher program showed an 8% higher rate of graduation among voucher students than among the voucher applicants who went to public school (77% versus 69%).

And studies have shown that the voucher schools have lower rates of violence.

As states continue to struggle with their budgets, in the face of ever-higher expenses for public services, the choice of increasing student outcomes by moving to vouchers is becoming more and more of a no-brainer—which is why during the last year, several states adopted or expanded voucher programs.

> *"Most students with vouchers can only afford to attend private or parochial schools that, in many cases, are only marginally less bad than their public schools."*

False Choice: How Private School Vouchers Might Harm Minority Students

Matthew McKnight

In the following viewpoint, Matthew McKnight argues that although school vouchers have been proposed as the solution to the problem of the education achievement gap along racial lines, the evidence does not support vouchers as the answer. McKnight claims that there are numerous problems with voucher programs, such as funding, which prevent vouchers being used for high-performing private schools without additional money. Furthermore, McKnight contends that voucher programs do not address the problems minority students face with respect to diversity and inclusion.

Matthew McKnight is a reporter for the New Yorker, *a weekly magazine of culture, criticism, and commentary.*

As you read, consider the following questions:

1. According to the author, in what year did the District of Columbia first implement the use of school vouchers?

2. McKnight claims that the maximum funding under the newly reinstated voucher program in Washington, DC, is what amount per year?

3. Instead of enacting school voucher programs, McKnight proposes spending public money on what?

For decades, policy wonks, lawmakers, and educators have wrestled with the phenomenon of the achievement gap in U.S. schools. The answer to the essential question—why does such a racialized gap exist?—has proven elusive. Race itself, poverty, location, lack of stability at home, and bad teachers has each been the culprit du jour at one time or another. Recently, however, many conservatives have decided that the problem might be the whole of public education—so they have sought to direct more funds toward private schools.

On March 31, the U.S. House of Representatives passed a bill to reinstate the school voucher program in the District of Columbia. The program delivers funding for low-income parents to send their children to private and independent schools. It was launched in 2003 as a five-year pilot but was discontinued by the Obama administration in 2009. (Students with vouchers were allowed to keep them until they graduated, but no new students could be enrolled in the program.) Although Obama continues to oppose the program, it was attached as a rider onto last week's House budget deal, which passed the Senate on Thursday [April 14, 2011]. The conventional wisdom among those—namely Republicans—backing the program's revival says that students with vouchers are all receiving top-notch educations, free of the problems that students at public schools face.

But there is growing evidence that suggests otherwise. There are problems with education in America that are so deeply rooted that not even private and independent schools escape them, which renders the notion of school vouchers out of touch with the nuanced problem of the achievement gap that it attempts to solve. It is worth giving a closer look to the real nature of the private-school environments where low-income children with vouchers often end up.

At face value, vouchers' main function—delivering choice to low-income parents with children in failing schools—seems like a laudable goal. Except, that is, when it doesn't work. In its most recent study of the D.C. Opportunity Scholarship Program (OSP), as the District's vouchers regime is called, the federal Department of Education's Institute of Education Sciences (IES) reported that there have been "no statistically significant impacts on overall student achievement in reading and math after at least four years." Patrick Wolf, the lead investigator on the study, ultimately supported OSP in his February testimony to the Senate Committee on Homeland Security and Governmental Operations. In the same testimony, however, he admitted that interpreting the program's effectiveness "is bound to be somewhat subjective."

Inadequate funding is part of the problem. In D.C., students who accepted vouchers before the program was discontinued generally attended one of two types of schools: parochial schools, and private or independent schools. But tuition at the city's most elite, highest-achieving private schools are far too expensive for both the previous voucher allotments ($7,500 per year) and the increase proposed in the new bill ($2,000 per year). A smaller number of students were able to make up the difference from other funding sources in order to attend the more costly private schools. But, this means that most students with vouchers can only afford to attend private or parochial schools that, in many cases, are only marginally less bad than their public schools.

The Voters' Choice: State Referenda on Vouchers

State	Year	Results
Maryland	1972	Rejected 55% to 45%
Michigan	1978	Rejected 75% to 26%
Colorado	1992	Rejected 67% to 33%
California	1993	Rejected 70% to 30%
Washington	1996	Rejected 64% to 36%
Michigan	2000	Rejected 69% to 31%
California	2000	Rejected 71% to 20%
Utah*	2007	Rejected 68% to 32%

* Voters in Utah repealed a program already created by the state legislature, as opposed to voting on a proposed program.

TAKEN FROM: Coalition for Public Schools, "Fact Sheet: The Case Against Private Schools Vouchers," www.coalition4publicschools.org, 2009.

Problems with voucher programs persist outside the District, too. In late March, Wisconsin's Department of Public Instruction released findings from the study of a similar program in Milwaukee that, when it began 21 years ago, was thought to be the standard-bearer for school choice programs. The *Journal Sentinel* reported, "Students in Milwaukee's school choice program performed worse than or about the same as students in Milwaukee Public Schools in math and reading on the latest statewide test, according to results released Tuesday that provided the first apples-to-apples achievement comparison between public and individual voucher schools."

But the flaws in voucher programs run deeper than what mere test scores can show. For many students who accept vouchers, there is a broader issue—the fact that private school education comes with its own sets of problems for minority students that proponents of vouchers either aren't aware of or choose not to acknowledge. Within the walls of many private schools, there are realities that create gaps between white students and low-income minority students.

These gaps have to do with a sense of inclusion. Psychologists Greg Walton and Geoffrey Cohen have dedicated years of study to the impact that the quality of a person's social connection has on his or her achievement. Their 2007 research paper concluded, "[I]t seems that Black students globalized the implications of social hardship into a conclusion about their potential to fit and succeed in an academic setting." More to the point, the authors wrote:

> We suggest that, in academic and professional settings, members of socially stigmatized groups are more uncertain of the quality of their social bonds and thus more sensitive to issues of social belonging. We call this state *belonging uncertainty*, and suggest that it contributes to racial disparities in achievement.

The study found no such results among Caucasian students. Rather, as shown by a more recent study that builds on Walton and Cohen's research, stereotypes, and feeling the risk that one might confirm stereotypes, also negatively influence performance among minorities. Barnard [College] Professor Steven Stroessner calls this "stereotype threat." He writes that, in performance-based situations in which a person actually is or expects to be "the single representative of a stereotyped group ... or a numerical minority," lowered performance results most often occur. Stroessner adds that "minority status is sufficient but not necessary for stereotype threat"; indeed, "a reminder of a stereotype ... or even just a reminder of a person's group membership (typically race or gender) that is tied to the stereotype" can be other factors.

Curious about real-life examples of this phenomenon, I talked to students, parents, and administrators at various private schools in D.C. Dominic Vedder, 17, an African American senior at the elite, private Sidwell Friends School in D.C., notices the impact of "belonging uncertainty" and "stereotype threat." He came to Sidwell in ninth grade from KIPP DC KEY, a public charter school and part of a nationwide network that has recently come under scrutiny; although Sidwell accepts vouchers, he is not the recipient of one. "Sometimes, especially if you haven't been at Sidwell for a long time, you can definitely get the feeling of [being] an outsider, because there are a lot of people who have been with each other since kindergarten," Vedder said. He also pointed to the sharp racial imbalances, among students and teachers, as obstacles to a successful transition to Sidwell. When asked how he overcame them—he admits the change of schools incited a drop in his grades—Vedder said, "I stay involved in school, hang out with my friends [after] school," and participate in extra-curricular activities. In other words, it was through great effort that he found success.

But it's not so easy for other minority students transferring from public into private schools, often with the help of vouchers, to find success. (And not all private schools, as previously mentioned, are nearly as excellent, academically and otherwise, as Sidwell.) Recently, the researchers intervened against "belonging uncertainty" by engaging black college freshmen in an hour-long exercise aimed at conveying that every student—regardless of race—faces uncertainty about belonging in a new community. They found that such interventions could reverse the impact that uncertainty has on a minority student's academic performance. Unfortunately, however, voucher programs don't always come equipped with interventions to help minority students transition into their new school environments.

To be sure, some private schools across the country work to improve diversity and inclusion, and should continue to do so. And, even when achievement gains aren't clear for students with vouchers, there may be other factors—such as parent satisfaction—that come into play when determining the best place to send children to learn.

But the fact remains that vouchers, including D.C.'s reviving program, generally ignore the factors that work directly against their success. The ultimate fallacy of vouchers is that they are designed to deliver choices, not outcomes. In that process, minority students stand a serious chance of losing out. It would be wise, instead, to devote public money and energy to creating thriving public schools, open to all students and focused on their achievement, regardless of background.

"In a tax-credit program . . . the amount is . . . defined entirely by the individual choice of the donating citizens."

In Defense of School-Choice Tax Credits

David French

In the following viewpoint, David French argues against the idea that school-choice tax credits cost the government money. French claims that unlike school vouchers, which use government funds, tax credits use private funds thereby avoiding any charge of harm to other taxpayers. French contends that tax credits would ultimately save the government money on the savings from expanding private schools. French is a senior counsel at the American Center for Law and Justice.

As you read, consider the following questions:

1. Why does French think it is misleading to say the "government ends up with less money" because of the tax-credit school-choice plan?

2. According to the author, who determines a citizen's total tax liability?

3. How does the government end up with more money under the Arizona tax-credit plan, according to the author?

Robert, I'm beginning to get the sense we're going to have to agree to disagree on the merits of Arizona's tax-credit school-choice plan. But before I let our little dispute pass into history, I've got to take issue with this statement:

> There is no difference between (A) having the government spend money on a program, and (B) having the government give dollar-for-dollar credits so that individuals can "donate" (i.e., divert their tax dollars) to that program. Either way, the government ends up with less money, the individual has not foregone a single dollar, and the program has more money.

I'm not quite sure how you can say there's "no difference." The differences are, in fact, vast—economically, fiscally, and conceptually. In every voucher program ever created, the vouchers represent an actual expenditure from the government treasury according to budgeted dollar amounts as limited by the specific appropriation. In a tax-credit program, by contrast, the direct money transfer is not from government to private citizen but from private citizen to private entity (the tuition organizations), and the amount is not a finite, budgeted amount but instead—like normal charitable contributions—defined entirely by the individual choice of the donating citizens. Thus, private choice defines the scope of the program. Whether the tuition organizations spend $50,000 or $50 million is up to the decisions of individuals, not the legislature.

Next, I think it's misleading to say the "government ends up with less money." There was considerable record evidence that the tax-credit program actually saved the government considerable money. If Arizona's private schools were to close tomorrow, vast state expenditures would be required to house

Public Opinion on School Tax Credits

A proposal has been made to offer a tax credit for educational expenses (fees, supplies, computers, and tuition) to low- and moderate-income parents who send their children to public and private schools. Would you favor or oppose such a proposal?

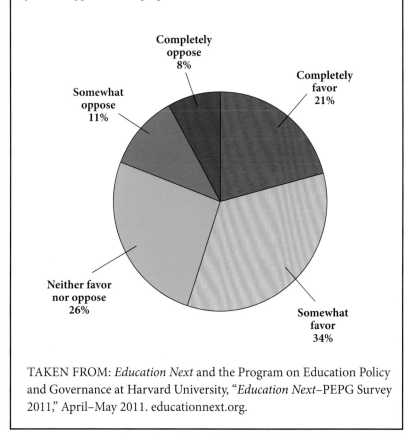

TAKEN FROM: *Education Next* and the Program on Education Policy and Governance at Harvard University, "*Education Next*–PEPG Survey 2011," April–May 2011. educationnext.org.

and educate tens of thousands of new students. The cost of the tax credit is far, far smaller than the cost of educating a child in an Arizona public school.

Finally, I love your phrase "divert their tax dollars." I prefer to describe it as being forced to pay less of their own money to the Arizona government. As Justice Kennedy himself said, "Private bank accounts cannot be equated with the Arizona State Treasury." The starting position for any citizen is that all the money they earn is theirs, not the state's, and then the individual determines their total tax liability (the portion of their money they pay to the government) according to applicable law. That law creates a marginal income-tax rate but also a myriad of deductions, credits, and other mechanisms that work together to define the actual tax dollars owed. Thus, the effective tax rate has long been quite different from the defined marginal rates, and I don't think it's accurate to define the difference as "diverted tax dollars." I don't think anyone would describe a lowered marginal tax rate or other tax cuts in that manner, so why define other—less sweeping—mechanisms that lower your tax liability as "diverted tax dollars?"

If I go to my neighborhood Super Walmart, and I carry with me a bundle of coupons, pick up an extra pack of Viva paper towels because of a two-for-one deal, and then bite the bullet and buy off-brand Four Loko instead of the real thing, I don't think of the savings as my "diverted grocery dollars." Instead, I just pay my grocery bill and am happy to have more money in my pocket.

Under the Arizona tax-credit plan, the government ends up with more money because of the vast cost savings inherent in expanded private education, individuals still pay actual money into the program in amounts they determine, and the program ends up with the amount of money the citizens want it to have. That's a plan conservatives can support.

"A . . . tuition tax credit program would harm public schools and local taxpayers."

Tax Credits for School Choice Do Not Benefit Taxpayers and Students

National Education Association

In the following viewpoint, the National Education Association (NEA) argues that the use of tax credits to fund parents' decisions to send children to private school is poor public policy. The NEA contends that the use of tax credits does not improve student performance and has a negative economic impact on public schools. The NEA also claims that the use of tax credits is an inequitable policy that benefits the wealthy, and it denies that individual taxpayers should be allowed choice in this area. The NEA is the nation's largest professional employee organization, with members working at every level of education, committed to advancing the cause of public education.

As you read, consider the following questions:

1. What two methods of using tax credits to offset the cost of private education does the author identify?

"Subsidizing Private Education at Taxpayer Expense," *National Education Association Policy Brief*, 2011, pp. 1–2. Copyright © 2011 by National Education Association. All rights reserved. Reproduced by permission.

2. What reason does the NEA give in support of its view that students who switch from public to private school because of tax credits will not save school districts money?

3. Identify one of the two analogies the NEA uses in support of its view that taxpayers should not get tax refunds for choosing to send their children to private school.

Efforts to subsidize private education take a variety of forms, with the most familiar being the private school voucher provided directly to parents. But there are other less direct ways governments subsidize private schools. One such method is to provide a tax credit to parents to offset their personal education expenses (education tax credit). Another is to allow individuals and corporations to reduce their tax bills by sending what they would otherwise owe in taxes to a foundation that turns the money into private school vouchers (tax credit voucher). Like directly funded vouchers, these tax loopholes do nothing to improve public schools, while actually reducing the amount of money available for proven school improvement strategies.

A Lack of Benefits from Tax Credits

Tax credit vouchers have *not* been proven effective in improving student academic performance. Research indicates that when student demographics are taken into account, public school students perform as well if not better than private school students. Students attending traditional public high schools are also just as likely to attend college as those attending private high schools.

Those who promote private school tax subsidies claim that the risk of losing students to private school forces public schools to improve. There is no credible research supporting this alleged positive competitive impact.

A common argument advanced in favor of private school tax credits is that they would save states money by encouraging families to switch from public schools to private ones. A study of individual tax credits in Arizona, however, showed that they were used primarily by families whose children already attended private school. In such cases, these programs represent net revenue losses for states.

Even in situations where students do switch from public school to private school, school districts may not experience savings, because districts cannot reduce their fixed costs—maintenance, utilities, debt service, transportation, etc.—in proportion to the number of students who leave. Rather than save money, school districts must make do with less.

The Problem of Inequity

A nationally recognized economic consulting firm determined that a proposed tuition tax credit program would harm public schools and local taxpayers, who would have to make up any funding shortfall resulting from reduced state expenditures and federal aid. Public school students would experience the most direct impact, as they would attend less well-funded schools or have to travel to distant public schools after neighborhood schools closed due to declining enrollment and funding.

As with most tax cuts, the financial benefits of education tax subsidies accrue primarily to the wealthy. In the case of an individual education tax credit, the financial benefits are enjoyed only by families that itemize their taxes, and can afford to pay tuition and then later reduce their tax bill by all or some of their costs. The fiscal benefits of tax credit vouchers are also enjoyed primarily by those who can afford to make donations to foundations that will use the money to grant vouchers. The foundations that convert charitable donations into vouchers are also treated differently than other charitable foundations. Because taxpayers receive credits against their tax bills for contributions to voucher foundations, rather than mere reductions of their taxable income, taxpayers seeking to maximize their charitable giving may favor voucher-granting foundations over other worthy causes.

To make private school tax subsidies politically palatable and less vulnerable to legal challenge, proponents often include in their proposals credits for public school expenses or contributions to public school extracurricular funds. Because families in less affluent communities cannot afford to make donations to their children's schools, the benefits of public school tax credits accrue primarily to wealthy school districts, increasing the disparities between rich and poor neighborhoods. The inclusion of provisions aimed at public school parents is more about making the proposals *appear* equitable than about actually providing public schools with equitable funding.

The Role of Taxes

Government provides public services for the benefit of *all* members of society. Taxpayers do not get to pick and choose which of these services their tax dollars will support, and which they would prefer not to fund. Taxpayers who buy books, for example, should not receive a tax rebate for not patronizing the public library. Nor should taxpayers who prefer country clubs to public golf courses receive rebates to compensate them for the additional cost of that private choice. Likewise, taxpayers who choose to send their children to private school should not receive tax refunds to pay tuition.

These private school tax subsidies increase the complexity of an already complex tax system. To claim an education tax credit, taxpayers must retain and submit receipts for all claimed education expenses. To minimize the risk of fraud in a tax credit voucher program, the state Department of Revenue would have to compare the contributions that taxpayers claim they made to voucher foundations with the receipts reported by those groups, and also confirm that the donations were used to fund vouchers that were actually used in eligible schools. In Arizona, the chief economist for the state Department of Revenue warned that the program contained "lots of possibilities for abuse."

Tax credit vouchers and education tax credits are just the latest in a long list of schemes that have diverted attention from what our children and our schools really need—programs and funding to recruit, train, and retain the best teachers; smaller classes so they can devote enough attention to each child; high-quality early childhood education programs so children come to school ready to learn; tutoring to ensure that those who fall behind aren't left behind, and the active involvement of parents and the community. All students deserve the right to a great public school, and it is with these kinds of investments—not education tax subsidies—that we will achieve this goal.

Periodical and Internet Sources Bibliography

The following articles have been selected to supplement the diverse views presented in this chapter.

Americans United for Separation of Church and State	"10 Reasons Why Private School Vouchers Should Be Rejected," February 2011. www.au.org/church-state/february-2011-church -state/featured/10-reasons-why-private-school -vouchers-should-be.
Robert J. Birdsell and Mary Claire Ryan	"Where Credit Is Due," *America*, November 28, 2011.
Lindsey Burke	"Why Market Forces Are Good for Education," *Atlantic*, February 3, 2012.
Michael Chingos and Paul Peterson	"The Effects of School Vouchers on College Enrollment," Brookings Institution, August 2012. www.brookings.edu/events/2012/08/23 -school-vouchers.
Lee Fang	"How Online Learning Companies Bought America's Schools," *Nation*, December 5, 2011.
Jack Jennings	"School Vouchers: No Clear Advantage in Academic Achievement," *Huffington Post*, July 27, 2011. www.huffingtonpost.com/jack-jennings/ school-vouchers-no-academic-advantage_b _909735.html.
Michael A. LaFerrara	"Toward a Free Market in Education: School Vouchers or Tax Credits?," *Objective Standard*, Spring 2011.
Paul E. Peterson	"Let the Charters Bloom," *Hoover Digest*, vol. 3, 2010.
Richard W. Rahn	"Put Department of Education in Timeout," *Washington Times*, November 3, 2010.
Katrina Trinko	"Why School Vouchers Are Worth a Shot," *USA Today*, April 19, 2011.

CHAPTER 3

Should Religion and Religious Ideas Be Part of Public Education?

Chapter Preface

The US Constitution protects religious freedom in the United States. The First Amendment to the Constitution states, "Congress shall make no law respecting an establishment of religion, or prohibiting the exercise thereof." The first portion, known as the establishment clause, prohibits the government from establishing any official religion. The second portion, known as the free exercise clause, prohibits the government from barring the exercise of religion. These clauses form the foundation of religious freedom in the United States, forbidding government from promoting any particular religion while also allowing people to practice any religion that they choose. Balancing these two principles in the public sphere can be challenging, and this tension is particularly evident in the public schools, where social battles over the role of religion have been ongoing for decades.

The First Amendment's guarantee of freedom from government establishment of religion and guarantee of free exercise of religion applies to the public schools. The US Supreme Court has held that the public school context is one in which government must be particularly careful about establishing or endorsing religion: "What to most believers may seem nothing more than a reasonable request that the nonbeliever respect their religious practices, in a school context may appear to the nonbeliever or dissenter to be an attempt to employ the machinery of the State to enforce a religious orthodoxy." (*Lee v. Weisman*, 505 US 577 [1992]). Over the last few decades the Court has concluded that public school officials may not engage in activities that endorse a particular religion—such as starting the day with a prayer, posting religious material, such as the Ten Commandments, in the classroom, or teaching creationism instead of evolution in science classes—to avoid violation of the establishment clause.

Although the Court has held that public school officials may not endorse religion, the Court has recognized that the free exercise clause of the First Amendment protects the rights of students to exercise their religion: "There is a crucial difference between government speech endorsing religion, which the Establishment Clause forbids, and private speech endorsing religion, which the Free Speech and Free Exercise Clauses protect." (*Board of Education of Westside Community Schools v. Mergens*, 496 US 226 [1990]). Thus, as long as student religious activity at school is private, it is protected. The US Department of Education clarifies that "students may read their Bibles or other scriptures, say grace before meals, and pray or study religious materials with fellow students during recess, the lunch hour, or other noninstructional time to the same extent that they may engage in nonreligious activities." However, the Department of Education also notes that student religious expression, as with other privately initiated student expression, may be limited when students are engaged in school activities and instruction, cautioning that "the Constitution mandates neutrality rather than hostility toward privately initiated religious expression."

History shows that even when the Supreme Court decides the issue, not everyone agrees with the outcome. This chapter demonstrates that debates about school prayer, Bible classes, and the teaching of intelligent design and creationism continue despite the fact that the Court has reached conclusions on these issues, as people disagree about the extent to which religion and religious ideas should be a part of public education.

| "History textbooks have been scrubbed
clean of religious references."

Public Schools Have Been Overly Sanitized of Religion

John W. Whitehead

In the following viewpoint, John W. Whitehead argues that attempts to keep religion out of school have gone too far. Whitehead claims that recent incidents show that an irrational understanding of the separation of church and state has led to a misguided belief that religion must be entirely expelled from public schools. Whitehead claims that America's history and founding support the view that public life ought to include many viewpoints, including religious ones.

John W. Whitehead is an attorney, author of The Rights of Religious Persons in Public Education, *and founder and president of the Rutherford Institute, which promotes civil rights, especially religious rights.*

As you read, consider the following questions:

1. According to the author, what two messages were conveyed to the public school student who was prevented from giving his presentation on Jesus to the entire class?

2. Whitehead says that secularists often cite what principle to justify the censorship of religious expression?

3. According to the author, what role did religion play in early public school curriculum in the United States?

Our young people are growing up in a world in which *God* is the new four-letter word. Look around and you will find that while it is permissible for children in many public school systems and homes to read novels with graphic language and watch sexually explicit commercials on TV, talking about God or religion is taboo.

Attacks on Religion in School

Few objections are raised over the kind of music kids are listening to on their MP3-players at school during non-instructional time. However, lawsuits are constantly being filed over whether students should observe a moment of silence at the start of the school day. Two incidents that perfectly illustrate my point recently came across my desk.

The first incident involves Wade, a fourth grader from Colorado. Wade's class was given a "Hero" assignment, which required each student to pick a hero, research the person and write an essay. The student would then dress up and portray the chosen hero as part of a "live wax museum" and give an oral report in front of the class.

However, when the 9-year-old chose Jesus as his hero, school officials immediately insisted that he pick another hero. (You have to wonder whether school officials would have objected had Wade chosen the Dalai Lama—or even the Rev. Martin Luther King Jr.—as his hero.) After Wade's parents objected, the school proposed a compromise: Wade could write the essay on Jesus. He could even dress up like Jesus for the "wax museum." However, he would have to present his oral report to his teacher in private, with no one else present, rather than in front of the classroom like the other students.

A Zero-Tolerance Attitude

In an attempt to avoid offending anyone, America's public schools have increasingly adopted a zero-tolerance attitude toward religious expression. . . . Such politically correct thinking has resulted in a host of inane actions, from the Easter Bunny being renamed "Peter Rabbit" to Christmas concerts being dubbed "Winter" concerts, and some schools even outlaw the colors red and green, saying they're Christmas colors. And . . . simply because someone is offended by the title, students cannot play music that has no words and is performed with no religious intent.

John W. Whitehead, Liberty,
January–February 2010.

The message to young Wade, of course, was two-fold: first, Jesus is not a worthy hero, and second, Jesus is someone to be ashamed of and kept hidden from public view. Yet do we really want our young people to grow up believing that freedom of speech means that you're free to talk about anything as long as you don't mention God or Jesus?

Wade is not the only school-aged child being singled out for censorship because of a particular religious viewpoint. For instance, a third grader at an elementary school in Las Vegas, Nevada, was asked to write in her journal about what she liked most about the month of December. When the child wrote that she liked the month of December because it's Jesus's birthday and people get to celebrate it, her teacher tapped her on the shoulder and informed her that she was not allowed to write about religion in school.

The Separation of Church and State

Much of the credit for this state of affairs can be chalked up to secularist organizations that have worked relentlessly to drive religion from public life. John Leo, a former contributing editor at *U.S. News and World Report*, painted a grim picture of those who operate under the so-called guise of safeguarding the separation of church and state so that all faiths might flourish. Leo's article, written seven years ago, was an eerie foreshadowing of our current state of affairs:

> History textbooks have been scrubbed clean of religious references and holidays scrubbed of all religious references and symbols. Some intellectuals now contend that arguments by religious people should be out of bounds in public debate, unless, of course, they agree with the elites.

> In schools the anti-religion campaign is often hysterical. When schoolchildren are invited to write about any historical figure, this usually means they can pick Stalin or Jeffrey Dahmer, but not Jesus or Luther, because religion is reflexively considered dangerous in schools and loathsome historical villains aren't. Similarly a moment of silence in the schools is wildly controversial because some children might use it to pray silently on public property. Oh, the horror. The overall message is that religion is backward, dangerous and toxic.

Unfortunately, as the many cases that I deal with demonstrate, things have only gotten worse since John Leo wrote those words. How do we explain why these instances of discrimination have become the rule, rather than the exception?

Plain and simple, an elite segment of society that views God as irrelevant has come to predominate. As Christopher Lasch details in his book *The Revolt of the Elites and the Betrayal of Democracy* (1995):

> Public life is thoroughly secularized. The separation of church and state, nowadays interpreted as prohibiting any public recognition of religion at all, is more deeply en-

trenched in America than anywhere else. Religion has been relegated to the sidelines of public debate. Among elites it is held in low esteem—something useful for weddings and funerals but otherwise dispensable. A skeptical, iconoclastic state of mind is one of the distinguishing characteristics of the knowledge classes. Their commitment to the culture of criticism is understood to rule out religious commitments. The elites' attitude to religion ranges from indifference to active hostility.

The Threat of Extreme Secularism

Those who have adopted this secular outlook frequently cite the "wall of separation between church and state" as justification for censoring, silencing and discriminating against religious individuals, especially in the public schools. The threat posed by this extreme secularism is that religion and religious people are not merely kept separate from the school system but are instead forced into a position of utter subservience.

Moreover, contrary to history and tradition, most Americans have now come to accept the assumption that religious faith has no real bearing on civic responsibility or morality. This is because the extreme concept of the separation of church and state has literally been drilled into their heads through the schools, the media and the courts.

This is not to say that the concept of a wall of separation between church and state is not an important part of our cultural and legal landscape. However, the wall of separation is not the issue in the myriad of cases that arise in schools today. The issue in such instances is the religious believer versus the secular state. It is also a denial of everything this country stands for in terms of the freedoms of speech, religion and a respect for moral traditions.

The History of Religion in America

Contrary to the propaganda peddled by various separatist organizations, those who founded this country were not antireligionists. Take Thomas Jefferson, for example, who coined the *wall of separation* phrase. While Jefferson was correct in arguing that churches should not interfere in the workings of government, he did not intend to seal religion off hermetically from public life. In fact, Jefferson was a religious person who on two separate occasions—once while President—reduced the New Testament to include what he believed were the true teachings of Jesus (absent the virgin birth and the miracles). Jefferson's conclusion was that Jesus' teachings were "the most sublime and benevolent code of morals which has ever been offered to man."

American public education was established on the precept that it would accommodate religion. For example, the Northwest Ordinance, enacted by the Continental Congress in 1787, recognized the importance of religion in its provision setting aside federal property for schools. This section of the Ordinance provided: "Religion, morality, and knowledge being essential to good government and the happiness of mankind, schools and the means of education shall forever be encouraged." Thus, according to the Northwest Ordinance, religion was part of the foundation of American public schools.

In fact, the historical record reveals that religion was integrated into the early public school curriculum. Textbooks referred to God without embarrassment, and public schools considered one of their major tasks to be the development of moral character through the teaching of religion.

While the cultural landscape has changed greatly since the founding of the country, one thing has not: America still stands for freedom and pluralism. What this demands is an equal voice for all viewpoints. This includes religion. If we do not maintain this ideal, then the only alternative is a form of secular society and government that respects no one's freedom or opinions at all.

| "Neutrality is the appropriate stance for the government to take toward religion."

Public Schools Are Rightfully Neutral on Religion

Americans United for Separation of Church and State

In the following viewpoint, the organization Americans United for Separation of Church and State argues that disallowing religious promotion in public school while protecting individual student religious expression is the correct approach in a religiously diverse country. The author contends that despite much misunderstanding, religion has not been purged from the school realm but only government sponsorship of it.

Americans United for Separation of Church and State is a nonpartisan educational organization dedicated to preserving the constitutional principle of church-state separation.

As you read, consider the following questions:

1. According to the author, did the US Supreme Court decision in *Engel v. Vitale* (1962) forbid students from praying at school at any time?

2. Are teachers allowed to use the Bible in class, according to Americans United for Separation of Church and State?

3. What two historical incidents does the author cite in support of the view that neutrality was the logical outcome of the history of religion in American schools?

Few issues in American public life engender more controversy than religion and public education. Unfortunately, this topic is all too often shrouded in confusion and misinformation. When discussing this matter, it's important to keep in mind some basic facts.

Ninety percent of America's youngsters attend public schools. These students come from homes that espouse a variety of religious and philosophical beliefs. Given the incredible diversity of American society, it's important that our public schools respect the beliefs of everyone and protect parental rights.

The schools can best do this by not sponsoring religious worship. This principle ensures that America's public schools are welcoming to all children and leaves decisions about religion where they belong: with the family.

Prayer in Public School

The U.S. Supreme Court has been vigilant in forbidding public schools and other agencies of the government to interfere with Americans' constitutional right to follow their own consciences when it comes to religion. In 1962, the justices ruled that official prayer had no place in public education.

This decision is widely misunderstood today. The court *did not* rule that students are forbidden to pray on their own; the justices merely said that government officials had no business composing a prayer for students to recite. The *Engel v. Vitale* case came about because parents in New York challenged a prayer written by a New York education board. These

Christian, Jewish and Unitarian parents did not want their children subjected to state-sponsored devotions. The high court agreed that the scheme amounted to government promotion of religion.

In the following year, 1963, the Supreme Court handed down another important ruling dealing with prayer in public schools. In *Abington Township School District v. Schempp*, the court declared school-sponsored Bible reading and recitation of the Lord's Prayer unconstitutional.

Since those rulings, a myth has sprung up asserting that Madalyn Murray O'Hair, a prominent atheist, "removed prayer from public schools." In fact, the 1962 case was brought by a group of New York parents who had no connection to O'Hair, and the 1963 case was filed by a Unitarian family from the Philadelphia area. O'Hair, at that time a resident of Baltimore, had filed a similar lawsuit, which the high court consolidated with the Pennsylvania case.

It is important to remember that in these decisions the Supreme Court did not "remove prayer from public schools." The court removed only *government-sponsored* worship. Public school students have always had the right to pray on their own as class schedules permit.

Bible Reading in Public School

Also, the Supreme Court did not rule against official prayer and Bible reading in public schools out of hostility to religion. Rather, the justices held that these practices were examples of unconstitutional government interference with religion. Thus, the exercises violated the First Amendment.

Nothing in the 1962 or 1963 rulings makes it unlawful for public school students to pray or read the Bible (or any other religious book) on a voluntary basis during their free time. Later decisions have made this even clearer. In 1990, the high court ruled specifically that high school students may form clubs that meet during "non-instructional" time to pray, read religious texts or discuss religious topics if other student groups are allowed to meet.

The high court has also made it clear, time and again, that objective study *about* religion in public schools is legal and appropriate. Many public schools offer courses in comparative religion, the Bible as literature or the role of religion in world and U.S. history. As long as the approach is objective, balanced and non-devotional, these classes present no constitutional problem.

In short, a public school's approach to religion must have a legitimate educational purpose, not a devotional one. Public schools should not be in the business of preaching to students or trying to persuade them to adopt certain religious beliefs. Parents, not school officials, are responsible for overseeing a young person's religious upbringing. This is not a controversial principle. In fact, most parents would demand these basic rights.

Religion in Public Education

A passage from the high court's ruling in the 1963 Pennsylvania case sums up well the proper role of religion in public education.

Justice Tom Clark, writing for the court, observed, "Nothing that we have said here indicates that such study of the Bible or of religion, when presented objectively as part of a secular program of education, may not be effected consistent with the First Amendment." Clark added that government could not force the exclusion of religion in schools "in the sense of affirmatively opposing or showing hostility to religion."

The court's ruling suggested simply that a student's family, not government, is responsible for decisions about religious instruction and guidance. There was respect, not hostility, toward religion in the court's ruling.

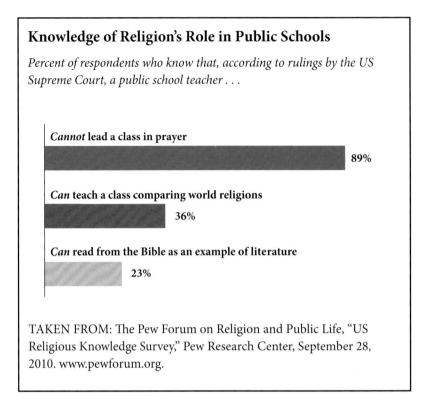

Knowledge of Religion's Role in Public Schools

Percent of respondents who know that, according to rulings by the US Supreme Court, a public school teacher . . .

***Cannot* lead a class in prayer**

89%

***Can* teach a class comparing world religions**

36%

***Can* read from the Bible as an example of literature**

23%

TAKEN FROM: The Pew Forum on Religion and Public Life, "US Religious Knowledge Survey," Pew Research Center, September 28, 2010. www.pewforum.org.

Justice Clark concluded, "The place of religion in our society is an exalted one, achieved through a long tradition of reliance on the home, the church, and the inviolable citadel of the individual heart and mind. We have come to recognize through bitter experience that it is not within the power of government to invade that citadel, whether its purpose or effect be to aid or oppose, to advance or retard. In the relationship between man and religion, the State is firmly committed to a position of neutrality."

A Logical Outcome of Neutrality

Some critics of the high court's rulings have suggested that these church-state rulings have no precedence in American history. On the contrary, the decisions are the logical outcome of a debate that has been under way in our country for many decades.

Public education for the masses, as conceived by Horace Mann and others in the mid 19th century, was intended to be "non-sectarian." In reality, however, schools often reflected the majority religious view, a kind of nondenominational Protestantism. Classes began with devotional readings from the King James Version of the Bible and recitation of the Protestant version of the Lord's Prayer. Students were expected to take part whether they shared those religious sentiments or not.

Catholic families were among the first to challenge these school-sponsored religious practices. In some parts of the country, tension over religion in public schools erupted into actual violence. In Philadelphia, for example, full-scale riots and bloodshed resulted in 1844 over which version of the Bible should be used in classroom devotions. Several Catholic churches and a convent were burned; many people died. In Cincinnati, a "Bible War" divided the city in 1868 after the school board discontinued mandatory Bible instruction.

Tensions like this led to the first round of legal challenges to school-sponsored religious activity in the late 19th century. Several states ruled against the practices. Compelling children to recite prayers or read devotionals from certain versions of the Bible, these courts said, was not the job of public schools. They declared government-imposed religion a violation of state constitutions and the fundamental rights of conscience. Eventually, the U.S. Supreme Court adopted this view as well, applying the church-state separation provisions of the First Amendment of the U.S. Constitution.

Guidelines for Religion in Schools

The high court's decisions have worked well in practice. In 1995, a joint statement of current law regarding religion in public schools was published by a variety of religious and civil liberties organizations. This statement served as the basis for U.S. Department of Education guidelines intended to alleviate concerns about constitutional religious activities in schools.

These guidelines, which were sent to every public school in the nation, stressed that students have the right to pray or to discuss their religious views with their peers so long as they are not disruptive. But the guidelines went on to state that public schools are prohibited from sponsoring worship or pressuring students to pray, meditate, read religious texts or take part in other religious activities.

These are common-sense guidelines, but they are not enough for some people. Misguided individuals and powerful sectarian lobbies in Washington continue to press for religious majority rule in the nation's public schools. They advocate for school prayer amendments and other measures that would permit government-sponsored worship in the schools. They want their beliefs taught in the public schools and hope to use the public schools as instruments of evangelism.

The Need for Religious Neutrality

Americans must resist these efforts. They must protect the religious neutrality of public education. Being neutral on religion is not the same as being hostile toward it. In a multi-faith, religiously diverse society such as ours, neutrality is the appropriate stance for the government to take toward religion. Under this principle, public schools can allow for individual student religious expression without endorsing or promoting any specific faith.

The United States has changed since its founding in 1787. A nation that was once relatively religiously homogeneous has become one of the most pluralistic and diverse on the face of the globe. Scholars count over 2,000 different denominations and traditions in our country.

The answer to disputes over religion in public schools is simple: Keep the government out of the private religious lives of students. Leave decisions about when and how to pray (or whether to pray at all) to the home. This is the course the Supreme Court has adopted, and we are a stronger nation for it.

As Supreme Court Justice Anthony Kennedy said in a June 1992 opinion, "No holding of this Court suggests that a school can persuade or compel a student to participate in a religious exercise. . . . The First Amendment's Religion Clauses mean that religious beliefs and religious expressions are too precious to be either proscribed or prescribed by the State."

| *"Secular humanism ... [is predomi-*
nant] in kids' school-day devotions."

The Ruling Religion in Schools

Kurt Williamsen

In the following viewpoint, Kurt Williamsen argues that al-
though displays of Christianity have been removed from the
public schools and other public places, other religions have not
suffered the same fate. Williamsen claims that the most domi-
nant religion taught in public schools is secular humanism,
which denies the existence of God but endorses a particular ethi-
cal system. Williamsen contends that the promulgation of secular
humanism is having dire consequences for society.

Kurt Williamsen is associate editor of the New American, *a*
publication of the conservative John Birch Society.

As you read, consider the following questions:

1. Williamsen claims that bans on public Christianity are meant to have what effect?

2. According to the author, what is the core moral teaching of secular humanism?

3. What premise are the statistics about children from fatherless homes, cited by the author, intended to support?

Christmas came again—along with the numerous lawsuits and public prohibitions against public displays of Christianity. Many agree with making Christianity invisible because the phrase "separation of church and state" is repeated so often that even school kids can recite it with little prompting.

But even aside from the fact that there is no such phraseology in the Constitution or Bill of Rights, that Congress has opened with a prayer since its inception, that several states had state religions, and that every state's constitution opens with praise to God, it's a ludicrous notion: As Christianity is heaved out of the public sphere, other religions take its place.

In fact, bans on public Christianity are strictly meant to eliminate Christian morals, not to adhere to the law. This should be obvious to anyone: While prayers are yanked from commencement ceremonies, and our Christian roots are removed from social studies/history classes, the Islamic religion is welcomed.

As Janet Levy at *American Thinker* noted, students at Excelsior Middle School in Discovery Bay, California, had to take Muslim names, recite Islamic prayers, and celebrate Ramadan. Carver Elementary in San Diego provided prayer time for Muslims, removed pork from menus, and segregated classes by gender. "The University of Michigan, a taxpayer-funded school, has provided separate prayer rooms and ritual foot baths, requiring bathroom modifications costing over $100,000, for Muslim observances." Also, the federal government is forcing the Berkeley, Illinois, school district to adjust its time-off policy so that a teacher may take a pilgrimage to Mecca during the school year. The list goes on.

And Islam is not even the dominant religion taught in public schools; "secular humanism"—which posits that humans are the central beings of the universe and that science, logic, and reason should be the basis for morality and deci-sion making—takes those honors in kids' school-day devo-tions.

Yes, secular humanism is a religion!

What is religion? It is any system of beliefs, practices, and ethical values underlying a code of behavior and a philosophy. (No, religion is not the "worship" of a supreme God; other-wise, Shintoism and Buddhism would not qualify as religions.) As part of "humanist" religious education, public schools teach that no family situation is inherently better than another and that morals are relative and should be reevaluated for each situation—essentially saying there is no absolute right or wrong (teaching ethics, of a sort). Schools eradicate God from any part in creation, inculcating kids with the idea that evolu-tion is how all species came about (teaching a belief system), and schools preach a creed of "social justice" that espouses a reverence for Mother Earth, fairness through government re-distribution, and a victim group mentality (teaching and insti-tuting personal practices).

In fact, U.S. courts have ruled that secular humanism is indeed a religion; they just somehow couldn't find it in the schools.

It should come as no surprise that a belief system initiated in schools through a reliance on illogic, falsehoods, ignorance, and political correctness propagates more of the same.

Here are several of hundreds of examples: Someone who states in schools that homosexuality is aberrant, high-risk be-havior would be punished severely as a bully and a bigot for demeaning homosexuals' beliefs—for making homosexuals feel bad about themselves—but disparaging Christian beliefs to Christian kids is somehow not a problem.

Secularists insist that youth have the freedom and encour-agement to experiment with sex—running a gauntlet of dis-ease and possible death—but also say that government should have the power to regulate equally personal decisions, such as what people eat and drink and what medical treatments they may receive.

And they teach that every type of family unit is equally desirable despite the fact that 63 percent of youth suicides are from fatherless homes, as are 90 percent of all homeless and runaway children, 85 percent of all children that exhibit behavioral disorders, and 80 percent of rapists motivated with displaced anger.

The children of cohabitating parents fare poorly as well, experiencing high rates of drug abuse, depression, physical and sexual abuse, and poverty, as well as dropping out of high school.

Ironically, as with all studies, undoubtedly, at least one scientific study somewhere will completely contradict these facts, which were gleaned from scientific studies. So much for the superiority and sanctity of science.

According to secularists, "reason" can provide societal guidance. Unfortunately without the prospect of divine retribution, too many find it logical and reasonable to lie and falsify to promote their beliefs.

When it comes to "a separation of church and state," it might be nice if people practiced what they preach.

> *"It's time that we scientists stopped acting like ... the theory of evolution ... was somehow inferior to creationism and intelligent design, and we could not win the competition for best ideas fairly and openly."*

Mr. Dawkins, Tear Down This Wall!

Satoshi Kanazawa

In the following viewpoint, Satoshi Kanazawa argues that creationism and intelligent design should be taught alongside evolution in schools in order to allow the ideas to compete fairly and openly. Kanazawa claims that he is not endorsing the teaching of creationism because he believes it is true but because he thinks it should be subjected to examination since so many people believe it. Kanazawa contends that to deny the open assessment of these theories in schools is akin to the failure of communist societies to properly teach the theory of capitalism. Satoshi Kanazawa teaches management at the London School of Economics in the United Kingdom.

Satoshi Kanazawa, "Mr. Dawkins, Tear Down This Wall! Why Creationism and Intelligent Design Should Be Taught in Schools," *Psychology Today*, March 22, 2009. Copyright © 2009 by Psychology Today. All rights reserved. Reproduced by permission.

As you read, consider the following questions:

1. According to Kanazawa, why did Communist political leaders not allow their citizens to be accurately exposed to the theory of capitalism?

2. What does Kanazawa believe will happen when an intelligent child is exposed to the theory of evolution and the theory of creationism?

3. The author infers that by failing to support the teaching of creationism and intelligent design, scientists are sending what message about evolution?

I am somewhat unusual as a scientist and evolutionary psychologist, in that I strongly support the teaching of creationism and intelligent design in schools. I personally don't understand why my fellow scientists in general and evolutionary psychologists in particular oppose it so vehemently. Perhaps it's because I'm old enough to remember (and to have been educated during) the Cold War.

It's sobering to recall that it is the 20th anniversary of the fall of the Berlin Wall this year, and that all of my undergraduate students were born into the world where there were no East and West Germany. To them, East and West Germanies are as historically quaint as East and West Roman Empires are to me. During the Cold War, we taught our children what capitalism was and what communism was, whereas children going to school in the Soviet Union and the rest of the Eastern Bloc countries never learned what capitalism was. They learned falsely negative views of capitalism and equally falsely positive views of communism. My wife was one of these children.

The communist political leaders did not allow their citizens to be exposed to accurate portrayals of capitalism because they knew, deep down, that anyone who learned what capitalism truly was would naturally opt for it instead of communism. They therefore could not allow their citizens to learn what it was. We, on the other hand, had no such worry, because we knew that anyone who carefully compared capitalism and communism would naturally opt for capitalism. We did not build a wall to keep our people in; anybody who wanted to emigrate to the Soviet Union was free to go. We had entry visas; they had exit visas. Communists had to build a wall to keep their people in, because they knew what would happen if they didn't. We all learned that they were right in October 1989. We won the Cold War, not because we didn't allow our citizens to learn about communism, but because capitalism was a genuinely superior economic and social system than communism.

No one who has a better idea or product is ever afraid of an open competition; politicians who can win a majority of the votes fairly and openly never rig the election. So why are scientists, who are supposed to be all for academic freedom of expression and thought, actively trying to suppress creationism and intelligent design in schools? Why are they afraid of an open competition? Why are they acting like Stalin or Mugabe?

Teach our children both evolution and creationism in schools. Any intelligent child who is confronted with comprehensive and accurate views of evolution and creationism will naturally opt for evolution. Those who don't and instead believe in creationism deserve to live in the dark. Not everybody deserves the truth.

Of course, there is the argument that we shouldn't teach creationism in schools because it is not true. It is true that it is not true. But then virtually everything they teach in the sociology and women's studies departments on every college campus throughout the world is false. Yet nobody is calling for sociology and feminism to be censored and banned from schools, and I for one would certainly not support such censorship. I believe anyone who wants to study sociology and women's studies should be entirely free to do so. Any intelligent student who is confronted with comprehensive and accurate views of evolutionary psychology and sociology will naturally opt for evolutionary psychology. Those who don't and instead believe in sociology deserve to live in the dark. Not everybody deserves the truth.

Another possible objection is the separation of church and state mandated by the Constitution. Maybe the Constitution needs to be amended slightly to allow the teaching of creationism in schools (although I personally don't think the teaching of creationism in public schools is a major breach of the separation of church and state). The Constitution is not a perfect, prescient document (after all, it's not the Bible!); that is why there have been so many amendments to it. Whether we like it or not, creationism—the fact that so many people believe in it, especially in the US—is a fact of life that we can neither change nor ignore. It is better to confront it head on and expose its flaws than to ignore it, hiding behind the Constitution. If we continue to ignore creationism in school, the children can never eliminate the possibility in their mind that it just might be true.

I think it's time that we scientists stopped acting like our product—the theory of evolution by natural and sexual selection—was somehow inferior to creationism and intelligent design, and we could not win the competition for best ideas fairly and openly. We should stop acting like the communists during the Cold War.

"Students . . . are not taught the critical thinking skills they need to evaluate questions about evolution and become good scientists."

Debate About Evolution Should Be Taught in Science Class

Casey Luskin

In the following viewpoint, Casey Luskin argues that it is necessary for science students to learn about some of the scientific doubts about the theory of evolution. Luskin claims that the push to teach evolution as settled fact amounts to a kind of censorship. He denies that debate about evolution needs to involve any endorsement of religion or religious theory and claims that attempts by proponents of evolution to paint it as such is disingenuous.

Casey Luskin is an attorney with the pro–intelligent design Discovery Institute and coauthor of Traipsing into Evolution: Intelligent Design and the *Kitzmiller v. Dover Decision.*

As you read, consider the following questions:

1. According to Luskin, what was the original reason for the controversy over the proposed biology textbooks in Louisiana?

2. Luskin claims that proponents of Darwinian evolution refer to scientific views that they dislike in what way?

3. The author claims that what fraction of Americans believe that students need to know about criticisms of evolutionary theory?

Critical inquiry and freedom for credible dissent are vital to good science. Sadly, when it comes to biology textbooks, American high school students are learning that stubborn groupthink can suppress responsible debate.

The Biology Textbook Controversy

In recent weeks [in December 2010], the media have been buzzing over a decision by the Louisiana State Board of Elementary and Secondary Education to adopt biology textbooks. A Fox News summary read "Louisiana committee rejects calls to include debate over creationism in state-approved biology textbooks. . . ." There was one problem with the story. Leading critics of evolution in Louisiana were not asking that public schools debate creationism, or even that they teach intelligent design. Rather, they wanted schools to simply teach the scientific debate over Darwinian evolution.

The controversy began because the biology textbooks up for adoption in Louisiana teach the neo-Darwinian model as settled fact, giving students no opportunity to weigh the pros and cons and consider evidence on both sides.

One textbook under review (*Biology: Concepts and Connections*) offers this faux critical thinking exercise: "Write a paragraph briefly describing the kinds of evidence for evolution." No questions ask students to identify evidence that

The Controversy About Evolution

While it is routinely asserted that the theory of evolution is no more controversial than the theory of gravity, this is mere bluster. The central claims of Darwinian evolution—that random mutation and natural selection (or some similarly unguided process) are sufficient to produce increasingly complex life forms—cannot be confirmed through experimentation in the way that the theory of gravity can be confirmed. Even if it were shown through experimentation that a Darwinian mechanism could produce a more complex life form from a simpler ancestor, it does not prove that this mechanism did *in fact* produce such an effect in the past. Explanations on the origins of complex life forms through Darwinian mechanisms will never approach the degree of certainty that one can have in other scientific concepts such as gravity, the heliocentric arrangement of the solar system, or Boyle's Law.

To assert that there is controversy over Darwinism is simply to state the obvious. Darwin's theory is controverted scientifically, and because of its implications, it remains controversial for purposes of public education.

David K. DeWolf,
"The 'Teach the Controversy' Controversy,"
University of St. Thomas Journal of Law & Public Policy,
Fall 2009.

counters evolutionary biology, because no such evidence is presented in the text. If the modern version of Charles Darwin's theory is as solid as most scientists say, textbooks shouldn't be afraid to teach countervailing evidence as part of a comprehensive approach. Yet students hear only the prevailing view.

A Subtle Form of Censorship

Is this the best way to teach science? Earlier this year a paper in the journal *Science* tried to answer that question, and found that students learn science best when they are asked "to discriminate between evidence that supports . . . or does not support" a given scientific concept. Unfortunately, the Darwin camp ignores these pedagogical findings and singles out evolution as the only topic where dissenting scientific viewpoints are not allowed.

Courts have uniformly found that creationism is a religious viewpoint and thus illegal to teach in public school science classes. By branding scientific views they dislike as "religion" or "creationism," the Darwin lobby scares educators from presenting contrary evidence or posing critical questions—a subtle but effective form of censorship.

The media fall prey to this tactic, resulting in articles that confuse those asking for scientific debate with those asking for the teaching of religion. And Darwin's defenders come off looking like heroes, not censors.

Those who love the First Amendment should be outraged. In essence, the Darwin lobby is taking the separation of church and state—a good thing—and abusing it to promote censorship. But one can be a critic of neo-Darwinism without advocating creationism.

Valid Doubts About Evolution

Eugene Koonin is a senior research scientist at the National Institutes of Health and no friend of creationism or intelligent design. Last year [in 2009], he stated in the journal *Trends in Genetics* that breakdowns in core neo-Darwinian tenets such as the "traditional concept of the tree of life" or "natural selection is the main driving force of evolution" indicate that the modern synthesis of evolution "has crumbled, apparently, beyond repair."

Likewise, the late Phil Skell, a member of the US National Academy of Sciences, considered himself a skeptic of both intelligent design and neo-Darwinian evolution. He took issue with those who claim that "nothing in biology makes sense except in the light of evolution" because, according to Dr. Skell, in most biology research, "Darwin's theory had provided no discernible guidance, but was brought in, after the breakthroughs, as an interesting narrative gloss."

In a 2005 letter to an education committee in South Carolina, Skell wrote: "Evolution is an important theory and students need to know about it. But scientific journals now document many scientific problems and criticisms of evolutionary theory and students need to know about these as well."

The Need for Debate

Skell was right, and polls show that more than 75 percent of Americans agree with him. The Louisiana textbook debate reflects the public's gross dissatisfaction with the quality of evolution instruction in biology textbooks.

The Louisiana Board should be applauded for rejecting censorship and adopting the disputed textbooks despite their biased coverage of evolution. Students need to learn about the evidence supporting the evolutionary viewpoint, and the textbooks present that side of this debate. But the books themselves should not be praised because they censor from students valid scientific questions about neo-Darwinian concepts—concepts that are instead taught as unquestioned scientific fact.

Students are the real losers here, because they are not taught the critical thinking skills they need to evaluate questions about evolution and become good scientists. When we start using the First Amendment as it was intended—as a tool to increase freedom of inquiry and promote access to scientific information—then perhaps these divisive controversies will finally go away.

"The fallout from this decades-long campaign to dismantle evolution education and re-insert religious ideology into public school science classes is substantial and disturbing."

Neither Creationism nor Debate About Evolution Should Be Taught in Schools

Heather Weaver

In the following viewpoint, Heather Weaver argues that attempts by creationists to influence science curricula should be resisted. Weaver contends that there is a long history of attempts to teach creationism in public schools, including recent attempts to teach intelligent design and to manufacture controversy about evolution where none exists. Weaver claims that the campaign is silencing teachers and harming science education.

Heather Weaver is a staff attorney for the American Civil Liberties Union Program on Freedom of Religion and Belief.

As you read, consider the following questions:

1. In what year and in what state was a law passed, later found unconstitutional, that prohibited the teaching of evolution, according to the author?

Heather Weaver, "Saving Souls," *Index on Censorship*, vol. 40, no. 4, November 2011, pp. 87–92, 94–95, 97–98. Index on Censorship is the world's leading free speech magazine. Subscribe here: www.indexoncensorship.org/subscribe.

2. In what year did the US Supreme Court strike down a law that required the teaching of creationism alongside evolution, according to Weaver?

3. The author cites a poll finding that what percentage of Americans believe that most scientists do not endorse evolution as a valid scientific principle?

In 1925, the Tennessee Legislature passed the Butler Act, a law that prohibited public school employees from teaching 'any theory that denies the Story of the Divine Creation of man as taught in the Bible', including any theory 'that man has descended from a lower order of animals'. The statute led to the prosecution and conviction later that year of John T. Scopes, a high school biology teacher who dared to discuss evolution with his students. Scopes was represented by the American Civil Liberties Union (ACLU), a then relatively new organisation dedicated to preserving individual rights and liberties guaranteed by law. The proceedings—dubbed the 'Scopes Monkey Trial' by the media—attracted international attention, and the conviction was ultimately overturned. The Tennessee law was never enforced again and similar evolution bans across the country were, over a number of decades, defeated.

The Teaching of Evolution

Eighty-six years later, the teaching of evolution is no longer a criminal act in any state. Indeed, though an organised movement of creationists has doggedly pursued various strategies to gain judicial approval for anti-evolution laws and other policies that seek to inject creationist beliefs into public school science curricula, American courts have repeatedly ruled that it is unlawful to censor the teaching of evolution in public schools or to use those schools to promote religious doctrine such as creationism. Despite its spectacular losses in the courts of law, however, the creationist movement marches on, and there is troubling evidence that it is growing increasingly successful in the court of public opinion, the political arena and public school classrooms.

Earlier this year [2011], for example, the ACLU received a complaint from the parent of a fifth-grade student at an Alabama public school. His daughter's teacher had abruptly halted a science lesson after the topic of evolution had come up in the class textbook. The teacher announced that she would not read or discuss the issue further because 'some of us believe in God' and 'some of us believe that the world was made in seven days and that God created man and the trees'. When the ACLU pressed the school district regarding the incident, officials dismissed the teacher's actions as a 'stray comment' and claimed that they follow all state educational guidelines, which include teaching biological evolution. The ACLU continues to investigate the incident and is seeking documents that might help show whether, in fact, the school district's teachers are censoring evolution lessons in science classes. If so, however, they would scarcely be alone.

A study published in *Science* last January [2011] showed that only 28 per cent of US public high school biology teachers provide adequate instruction in evolution. According to the study, which was based on a national survey of public high school biology teachers, 13 per cent of teachers 'explicitly advocate creationism or intelligent design by spending at least one hour of class time presenting it in a positive light'. The remaining 60 per cent 'fail to explain the nature of scientific inquiry, undermine the authority of established experts, and legitimise creationist arguments'. As appears to be the case with the Alabama school teacher who refused to continue with her science lesson, many teachers within this failing 60 per cent no doubt intentionally undermine the teaching of evolution because they perceive it as conflicting with their personal religious views.

The Creationists' Tactics

Many other teachers, however, merely want to avoid contro-versy and a backlash from students and parents, according to the study's authors, Penn State University political scientists Michael Berkman and Erik Plutzer. As Plutzer explained to Ars Technica, a science and technology news website: 'The challenge is for these teachers to stay out of trouble. They have to teach in a cautious way to avoid complaints from ei-ther side. They want to avoid what everyone wants to avoid, which is being called to the principal's office.' With polls show-ing that more than two-thirds of Americans support teaching creationism in public schools—either as a replacement for or alongside evolution—it is not surprising that this caution has led to instruction that not only understates the scientific case for evolution but also gives credence to and endorses creation-ist religious beliefs.

Creationist leaders are well aware of their success on this front and will not ease the pressure on teachers any time soon. They blame the discoveries of modern science, especially evolution, for destroying traditional notions of both God and man, giving rise to moral relativism, and thereby causing a host of societal ills. For them, then, the fight against evolution is a central battle in the so-called culture wars; it is a fight to reclaim our humanity and save our souls by restoring America and Americans to God. With the stakes so high, creationists will thus continue to do whatever they must to suppress the teaching of evolution in public schools, no matter the cost; and in light of the courts' refusal to sustain outright attacks on evolution or permit teaching creationism alongside it, that means targeting teachers directly and indirectly.

Among other tactics employed in recent years, creationists have sponsored a barrage of proposed laws that would autho-rise teachers to introduce fabricated 'weaknesses' of evolution into individual science classes. They have also launched a

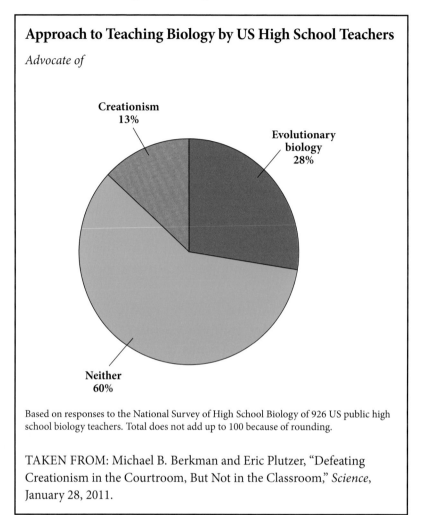

Approach to Teaching Biology by US High School Teachers

Advocate of

Creationism
13%

Evolutionary
biology
28%

Neither
60%

Based on responses to the National Survey of High School Biology of 926 US public high school biology teachers. Total does not add up to 100 because of rounding.

TAKEN FROM: Michael B. Berkman and Eric Plutzer, "Defeating Creationism in the Courtroom, But Not in the Classroom," *Science,* January 28, 2011.

high-profile anti-evolution propaganda campaign. These tactics aim to popularise creationist doctrine and anti-evolution beliefs. They ultimately seek to fashion a cultural environment that further emboldens willing teachers to flout the law by teaching creationism outright, while the remaining teachers are bullied into presenting students with incomplete and inaccurate information about evolution. Unfortunately, if the *Science* study is any indication, these tactics appear to be working.

The History of the Creationist Movement

To grasp just how insidious the creationist movement has become, it is helpful to understand its history. As Eugenie Scott and Nicholas Matzke of the National Center for Science Education chronicle in their 2007 paper, 'Biological Design in Science Classrooms', significant opposition to evolution education began in the 1920s 'as a by-product of the acrimonious split of American Protestantism into "fundamentalist" and "modernist" camps'. While modernists treated the Bible as 'allegorical and a product of human history', fundamentalists adopted 'a strict doctrine of biblical inerrancy, wherein the entire text of the Bible was considered to be divinely inspired truth and without error (and usually, but not always, to be interpreted literally)'.

Fundamentalists' original focus on evolution education in the public schools makes even more sense for the contemporary creationist movement. Thanks to mandatory attendance laws, the public schools offer access to a wide audience of students and families, including those of other faiths and non-believers. By targeting students in elementary and secondary school, creationists reach children when they are most impressionable and likely to internalise religious beliefs. By delivering religious doctrine through trusted teachers, they increase the likelihood that students will be less resistant to or questioning of religious doctrine, especially where, as is often the case today, the religious doctrine is cloaked in pseudo-science terms.

But the advantages of this approach are the very factors that have doomed it under the law. The First Amendment of the US Constitution contains the 'Establishment Clause', which prohibits the government from promoting or advancing religion. The US Supreme Court, the highest court in the country, has been particularly vigilant about enforcing this principle in public schools because of compulsory attendance laws, the vulnerability of children, and the special trust that families place in the government to educate their children with exploiting that opportunity to religiously indoctrinate them. As a result, the Supreme Court and lower courts have repeatedly rejected both efforts to incorporate instruction in creationism, creation-science, and intelligent design into public school curricula and efforts to undermine the teaching of evolution because of its perceived conflict with the Bible. After each judicial defeat, however, creationists have adapted their tactics and unrepentantly pressed forward, prompting many to comment on the irony of an evolving anti-evolution movement.

Defense of Evolution in the Courts

Though the Scopes Trial shone a light on the exploitation of the public schools to promote creationism and censor teaching about evolution, due to the fundamentalist movement and laws such as the Butler Act, evolution education in secondary public schools largely ground to a halt for several decades. It was not, as Scott and Matzke note, until the 50s and 60s— when fears arose that the country was falling behind the Soviet Union in technology and science—that evolution was reintroduced into many public school curricula via federally funded and commissioned textbooks written by scientists.

That effort was helped along by a 1968 Supreme Court decision [*Epperson v. Arkansas*] overturning a state ban on teaching evolution in public schools. Susan Epperson, a tenth grade biology teacher at Little Rock Central High School, challenged the Arkansas law, which prohibited public school teachers from teaching, or using textbooks that teach, human evolution. Much to the dismay of fundamentalists, the Supreme Court agreed that the law was an unconstitutional 'attempt to blot out a particular theory because of its supposed conflict with the biblical account, literally read'.

The events of the 50s and 60s, as well as the *Epperson* ruling, prompted supporters of creationism to alter their approach. They next tried to dress up their religious belief as 'creation-science' and mandate that it be given 'equal time' alongside evolution in science classes. The Supreme Court once again rebuffed the attempt to suppress evolution teaching and promote creationism. In 1987, [in *Edwards v. Aguillad*] the Court struck down Louisiana's Balanced Treatment for Creation-Science and Evolution-Science in Public School Instruction Act. The law forbade the teaching of evolution in public schools unless accompanied by instruction in creation-science. The Court ruled that the 'state may not constitutionally prohibit the teaching of evolution in the public schools, for there can be no non-religious reason for such a prohibition'. Nor, the court added, could the state require 'the presentation of a religious viewpoint that rejects evolution in its entirety'.

The Intelligent Design Movement

Unable to banish evolution from public school classrooms and barred from using public schools to promote creationism, the creationist movement shifted course again, claiming to have developed a new scientific theory to rival evolution: so-called 'intelligent design', which posits that nature is so irreducibly complex that it must have been created by an 'intelligent designer'. In 1998, the Discovery Institute, a leading purveyor of intelligent-design creationism, produced a document detailing its plan to use intelligent design theory to drive a 'wedge' into the scientific community, combat the growing acceptance of evolution in America, and 'replace it with a science consonant with Christian and theistic convictions'. Key prongs of the wedge strategy included: (1) producing 'solid' scholarship, research and argument (2) formally integrating teaching about intelligent design into public school science standards and curricula and (3) popularising design theory among influential leaders, the media, and in the 'broader culture'.

The movement never came close to reaching the first goal: intelligent design proponents were unable to produce any credible scientific research to buttress their belief. In addition, the campaign to formally incorporate intelligent design into public school curricula as a legitimate alternative to evolution also failed after a federal judge ruled in [2005] that intelligent design is just another extension of creationism, there is no scientific evidence to support it, and it cannot be taught in public schools. . . .

After the court's ruling in [*Kitzmiller v.*] *Dover*, creationism advocates were again forced to adapt their legal strategies. Their hopes of formally incorporating creationism, via intelligent design theory, into public school curricula dashed, they turned to subtler, more indirect ways to undermine evolution education. Drawing on intelligent design theory's argument that evolution contains 'gaps' in information, they have increasingly focused on the claim that there is controversy in the scientific community regarding the purported 'strengths and weaknesses' of evolutionary theory. They attack those who oppose incorporating this alleged controversy into science curricula as trampling free speech and seeking to brainwash students against critical analysis of scientific matters.

A Campaign of Misinformation

Specifically, under the pretexts of protecting the academic freedom of those who question evolution and fostering students' critical thinking skills, creationism advocates have been instrumental in proposing a number of state laws that would encourage and authorise public school teachers to present the so-called 'weaknesses' of evolution and other purportedly controversial scientific theories, such as global warming. More than 40 bills of this type have been proposed in 13 states over the past seven years. Creationists have also sought to inject the 'weaknesses' argument into state science educational standards, which govern public school science curricula and textbook approval processes.

The invocation of 'academic freedom' and 'critical analysis' to defend and advance a campaign singularly aimed at censoring proven scientific principles and promoting, in their stead, untested and unverifiable religious ideology would be laughable if it weren't for the serious risk that these tactics pose to sound science education. As Judge [John] Jones so artfully laid out in the *Dover* case, there is, of course, no controversy in the scientific community about the soundness of evolution as a scientific principle any more than there is a dispute over the validity of the theory of gravity. The purported 'weaknesses' that sponsors of these measures hope will be presented to students are recycled claims—universally rejected by scientists—that have been made for years by creationism and intelligent design advocates. There is no academic freedom in the right to provide demonstrably false information to students, and ensuring that information presented in science classes meets basic, well-established scientific standards enhances students' ability to engage in critical analysis.

Fortunately, due to strenuous opposition by the ACLU and other groups, nearly all of these legislative efforts have, thus far, been defeated. (Louisiana remains the only state to have passed an 'academic freedom' bill—the Louisiana Science Education Act.) But the campaign of misinformation has nevertheless been remarkably effective in confusing the public about the scientific support for evolution. While 57 per cent of Americans believe that humans and other living things have evolved over time, according to a poll conducted this September [2011] by the Public Religion Research Institute, only half (51 per cent) of those polled knew that there is also a broad scientific consensus supporting evolution. Over a quarter of respondents erroneously believed that scientists are divided on the question, and a mind-boggling 15 per cent of those polled thought that most scientists do not endorse evolution as a valid scientific principle. Seizing on this confusion, creationists have, in recent years, ramped up their propaganda efforts to gain and solidify public support for their cause. . . .

The Creation of a Controversy

After trying for decades, with little success, to enact formal legal change that would censor the teaching of evolution and instead permit creationist beliefs to be advanced in public schools, creationists appear to be embracing another approach that targets teachers more indirectly. By spreading misinformation and propaganda about evolution and inflaming the public debate over it, they have managed to create a cultural environment in which some teachers feel inspired to violate the law on their own by teaching creation, and many others—cognisant of the potential backlash from parents and students who might otherwise, however wrongly, perceive the teachers as challenging or denigrating their religious beliefs by endorsing evolution as a proven scientific concept—feel pressured to self-censor their science lessons.

Even the current legal strategies (relating to evolution's so-called 'strengths and weaknesses') avoid any direct attacks on evolution or direct advocacy of creationism or intelligent design. Instead, creationists now seek to exploit teachers' instincts to avoid controversy by giving them legal cover to present information that will placate those who dispute evolution on religious grounds.

The fallout from this decades-long campaign to dismantle evolution education and re-insert religious ideology into public school science classes is substantial and disturbing. Nearly three-quarters of students are receiving an inadequate foundation in science education. As creationists ratchet up and hone their current strategies targeted at teachers, these figures may grow worse. Consequently, millions of students are and will continue to be ill-prepared for the rigours of higher education and less likely to pursue careers in scientific fields. Much like the mid-20th century, when we discovered that the country was falling behind the world in technology and science, the US continues to lag far behind other nations in science education: a 2009 study by the Organisation for Economic Co-operation and Development rated US science students in the bottom ten of the top 30 industrialised nations.

The Threat to Science Education

Creationists' treatment of evolution as opinion, rather than scientific fact, is also likely to encourage devaluing scientific discovery in other contexts as well. Indeed, global warming deniers have already hitched their wagons to the evolution 'debate' by casting global warming as another 'scientific controversy' about which science curricula should remain circumspect.

In addition to the serious harm caused to science education, the use of public schools to advance religious ideology infringes the constitutional rights of every student to be free from government-imposed religious indoctrination. It also usurps the rights of parents, not the government, to control the religious upbringing of their children. And it creates religious dissension that undermines a core function of the public school system, which, as one Supreme Court justice [Felix Frankfurter, in *McCollum v. Board of Education*] has observed, was '[d]esigned to serve as perhaps the most powerful agency for promoting cohesion among a heterogeneous democratic people' and must, therefore, be kept 'scrupulously free from entanglement in the strife of [religious] sects'.

Though the courts and legislatures have traditionally marked the frontline for combatting the creationist movement, the battlelines are shifting. Make no mistake, it remains important to defend those judicial victories and to ensure that no ground is yielded in the legal sphere. But to truly protect science education in US public schools, we also must look beyond the courts and devise strategies to ease the pressure on science teachers to self-censor or otherwise compromise their instruction in evolution—starting with a plan to open the public's eyes to the overwhelming evidence and support for evolution in the scientific community, the primacy of evolution as a fundamental principle of biology and science, and the importance of sound science to our individual and common welfare.

Periodical and Internet Sources Bibliography

The following articles have been selected to supplement the diverse views presented in this chapter.

Americans United for Separation of Church and State	"Praying for Legal Behavior: Why Teachers Should Not Be Preachers," *Church & State*, October 2010.
Jay Bookman	"Religion Better Off When Separate," *Atlanta Journal-Constitution*, October 6, 2009.
Kristin Friedrich	"Evolution's Non-Debate," *Natural History*, June 6, 2009.
David Harsanyi	"The More You Know: Should School Boards Silence the Debate over Evolution?," *Reason.com*, April 1, 2009. http://reason.com/archives/2009/04/01/the-more-you-know.
Wendy Kaminer	"The Devilish Details of School Prayer," *Atlantic*, January 30, 2012.
Lauri Lebo	"The *Scopes* Strategy: Creationists Try New Tactics to Promote Anti-evolutionary Teaching in Public Schools," *Scientific American*, February 28, 2011.
William R. Mattox Jr.	"Teach the Bible? Of Course," *USA Today*, August 17, 2009.
Martha McCarthy	"Beyond the Wall of Separation: Church-State Concerns in Public Schools," *Phi Delta Kappan*, June 2009.
Jeff Passe and Lara Willox	"Teaching Religion in America's Public Schools: A Necessary Disruption," *Social Studies*, May–June 2009.

CHAPTER 4

How Should the Education System Be Improved?

Chapter Preface

There is widespread agreement in America that there is room for improvement in the education system. A 2012 Gallup poll showed that only 5 percent of Americans believe public schools provide children with an excellent education, and only 8 percent of Americans report complete satisfaction with the quality of education that students receive from kindergarten through grade twelve. However, when attempting to decide exactly what improvements should be implemented, very little consensus exists.

Suggestions for improving the public schools abound: In an open-ended question posed by a 2009 Gallup poll, 17 percent of respondents suggested better-quality teachers; 10 percent urged a return to the basic curriculum of reading, writing, and arithmetic; 6 percent urged better school funding; 6 percent suggested a reduction in class size; 6 percent wanted better pay for teachers; 5 percent demanded more parental involvement; 4 percent wanted improved testing standards; 4 percent suggested better discipline; and 4 percent thought there should be more teachers. Other suggestions included school vouchers, more religion, better security, year-round school, and the abolition of teachers' unions.

While there is no limit to the number of improvements that may be implemented, given adequate public support and funding, the ability to reach some kind of consensus on what improvements are necessary may prove to be the biggest hurdle. Even in situations where there is broad consensus about the existence of a problem, there is not always widespread support to address that problem. In the forty-fourth annual *PDK/Gallup Poll of the Public's Attitudes Toward the Public Schools* in 2012, Phi Delta Kappa and Gallup reported that a whopping 97 percent of Americans agreed that improving the nation's urban schools was either very important or fairly important. Nonetheless, when the same Americans were asked whether they would be willing to pay more taxes to provide funds to improve the quality of the nation's urban public schools, only 62 percent said they would be willing. Even with a majority willing to spend more money, it is unclear whether any agreement could be reached about how the money should be spent.

Agreement on the existence of a problem may be the strongest area of consensus, as the viewpoints in this chapter demonstrate. Looking at the different proposals for education reform, it becomes clear that not only are there competing views about what reforms would result in improvement, suggestions for improvement are oftentimes completely contradictory. Such a lack of consensus threatens to thwart any efforts to improve the current US education system.

> *"While Washington spends huge sums on things that are education-related, the riches produce almost nothing of educational value."*

Federal Spending on Education Should Be Cut

Neal McCluskey

In the following viewpoint, Neal McCluskey argues that federal government spending on education should be drastically reduced. McCluskey contends that since the 1970s, spending on education has risen, with no positive educational outcomes to show for it. McCluskey claims that continued education spending by the federal government is driven by politics, not by results.

Neal McCluskey is the associate director of the Cato Institute's Center for Educational Freedom and author of Feds in the Classroom: How Big Government Corrupts, Cripples, and Compromises American Education.

As you read, consider the following questions:

1. According to McCluskey, by what percentage did federal spending on education per student increase from 1970 to 2006?

2. According to the author, by how much did reading scores on the National Assessment of Educational Progress increase from 1971 to 2008?

3. Total federal spending on education in the 2008–2009 academic year amounted to how much, according to McCluskey?

If President [Barack] Obama cares about restoring sanity to federal finances, he will demand deep cuts to education spending. That's right: In tonight's [January 25, 2011,] State of the Union address, he will call to axe most of Washington's educationally worthless outlays.

Unfortunately, Mr. Obama is likely to prove that he doesn't care all that much about attacking the nation's crushing debt. According to several sources, he'll not only place education spending off limits, he might make increasing it a focal point of tonight's address.

Federal Spending on Education

But wait: Debt or no debt, isn't having an educated citizenry crucial to the nation's future? Isn't he right to protect education funding?

Education is, indeed, very important. But while Washington spends huge sums on things that are education-related, the riches produce almost nothing of educational value. If anything, the feds keep stuffing donuts into an already obese system.

Federal elementary and secondary education spending has risen mightily since the early 1970s, when Washington first started immersing itself in education. In 1970, according to the federal *Digest of Education Statistics*, Uncle Sam spent an inflation-adjusted $31.5 billion on public K–12 education. By 2009 that had ballooned to $82.9 billion.

On a per-pupil basis, in 1970 the feds spent $435 per student. By 2006—the latest year with available data—it was

Federal On-budget Funding for Education by Category

Selected fiscal years, in billions of constant fiscal year 2010 dollars

Year	Total	Elementary/ Secondary	Post- secondary	Other education	Research at educational institutions
1965	$36.9	$13.5	$8.3	$2.6	$12.6
1975	$90.5	$41.2	$29.7	$6.2	$13.3
1980	$89.7	$41.7	$28.9	$4.0	$15.1
1985	$74.6	$32.3	$21.4	$4.0	$16.9
1990	$84.7	$36.1	$22.4	$5.6	$20.7
1995	$100.6	$47.2	$24.7	$6.6	$22.0
2000	$110.0	$56.1	$19.2	$7.0	$27.7
2009	$165.8	$89.6	$37.0	$8.3	$30.8

Note: Detail may not sum to totals because of rounding

TAKEN FROM: Thomas D. Snyder and Sally A. Dillow, "Digest of Education Statistics 2010," National Center for Education Statistics, US Department of Education, April 2011.

$1,015, a 133 percent increase. And it's not like state and local spending was dropping: Real, overall, per-pupil spending rose from $5,593 in 1970 to $12,463 in 2006, and today we beat almost every other industrialized nation in education funding.

Higher Costs Without Results

What do we have to show for this?

Certainly more public school employees: Between 1969 and 2007, pupil-to-staff ratios were close to halved. Not coincidentally, these same people politick powerfully for ever more spending and against reforms that will challenge their bloated monopoly. They also routinely defeat efforts to hold them accountable for results.

This constant feeding of special interests is why we've gotten zilch in the outcome that really matters—learning. Since the early 1970s, scores on the National Assessment of Educational Progress—the "Nation's Report Card"—have been utterly stagnant for 17-year-olds, our schools' "final products." In 1973 the average math score was 304 (out of 500). In 2008 it was just 306. In reading, the 1971 average was 285. In 2008 it was up a single point, hitting 286.

The higher education tale is much the same, especially for student aid, the primary college dumping ground for federal dollars. According to the College Board, in 1971 Washington provided $3,814 in inflation-adjusted aid per full-time equivalent student. By 2009–10 that figure had more than tripled, hitting $12,894.

By most available indicators this has been money down the drain. For instance, only about 58 percent of bachelor's seekers finish their programs within six years, if at all. Literacy levels among people with degrees are low and falling. And colleges have raised their prices at astronomical rates to capture ever-growing aid.

Political Reasons for Continued Spending

What's the total damage?

It's impossible to know exactly because so many federal programs touch on education, but the *Digest* provides a decent estimate. In the 2008–09 academic year, Washington spent roughly $83 billion on K–12 education and $37 billion on higher education. (The latter, notably, excludes student-loan funds that fuel the tuition skyrocket but generally get repaid, as well as federally funded research conducted at universities.) Add those together and you get $120 billion, a sum that's doing no educational good and, therefore, leaves no excuse for not applying it to our $14 trillion debt.

And yet, it seems President Obama will not only protect education spending, he might fight to increase it. Why?

He could certainly believe that huge spending on education is a good thing. That, though, might mean he hasn't looked at all at what we've gotten for our money.

Unfortunately, it might also be that education is the easiest of all issues through which to buy political capital, whether from special interests like teachers' unions, or busy parents who don't have time to research what education funds actually produce. It's also ideal for demonizing opponents who might demand discomfiting fiscal discipline.

Of course, misguided intentions and political exploitation have been at work for decades in education, so this isn't new. We are now well past the point where we can ignore results. Today, we simply cannot afford to keep throwing money away.

> *"The kids who have the greatest need for public education are suffering the deepest cuts."*

Federal Spending on Education Should Not Be Cut

Robert L. Borosage

In the following viewpoint, Robert L. Borosage argues that in the wake of the economic recession, cuts in education are unfair and dangerous. Borosage claims that research shows the importance of funding early childhood education and a wide variety of educational programs. He contends that the calls by politicians for increased educational quality while states are slashing budgets constitute empty rhetoric.

Robert L. Borosage is the founder and president of the Institute for America's Future and codirector of its sister organization, the Campaign for America's Future.

As you read, consider the following questions:

1. According to the author, how many states have eliminated funding for pre-kindergarten programs?

2. Borosage cites a study finding that school budgets have been cut in how many states?

3. The author claims that since 1929, significant spending on education has only happened during what two events?

Wall Street's excesses blew up the economy. Now the question is who pays to clean up the mess. Across the country, our children are already paying part of the bill—as their schools are hit with deep budget cuts. A new report—*Starving America's Public Schools: How Budget Cuts and Policy Mandates Are Hurting Our Nation's Students*—released today [October 13, 2011,] by the Campaign for America's Future and the National Education Association, looks at five states to detail what this means to kids in our public elementary and secondary schools. (Full disclosure: I co-direct the Campaign.) The findings are sobering.

The Importance of Education

Every study shows the importance of early childhood education. Analysts at the Federal Reserve discovered that investments in childhood development have, in the words of Fed Chair Ben Bernanke, such "high public as well as private returns" that the Fed has championed such investments to noting they save states money by reducing costs of drop outs, special education, and crime prevention. Yet across the country, states are slashing funding for pre-kindergarten and even rolling back all-day kindergarten. Now pre-K programs serve only about one-fourth of 4-year-olds. Ten states have eliminated funding for pre-K altogether, including Arizona. Ohio eliminated funding for all-day kindergarten.

Every parent and teacher knows the importance of smaller classes, particularly in the early years when individual attention is vital. Yet across the country, schools have cut some 270,000 jobs since 2007 and are facing layoffs of nearly 250,000

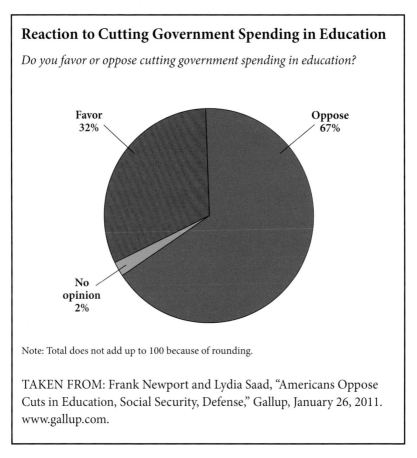

Reaction to Cutting Government Spending in Education

Do you favor or oppose cutting government spending in education?

Favor
32%

Oppose
67%

No
opinion
2%

Note: Total does not add up to 100 because of rounding.

TAKEN FROM: Frank Newport and Lydia Saad, "Americans Oppose Cuts in Education, Social Security, Defense," Gallup, January 26, 2011. www.gallup.com.

public school workers next year, many of them teachers. In Chester Upland, Pa., 40% of the teachers were eliminated, with class sizes rising from 21 to 30 in elementary schools and to 35 in high schools, causing students to walk out.

Intelligence comes in many forms. Successful schools offer a well-rounded curriculum—not just the basics, but art and music, social studies, extra-curricular activities, physical education. But now schools across the country are forced to terminate or charge extra for anything beyond the core curriculum. In York, Pa., art, music and physical education was eliminated in elementary schools. In Medina, Ohio, students returned to find courses in French, German, art, music, and Advanced Placement Science and Math were eliminated.

The Slashing of State Budgets

And children, needless to say, are extremely diverse. They learn in different ways, at different rates, and face different challenges. Public schools educate the poor and the affluent, those with developmental challenges and those who are gifted. Yet across the country, schools are slashing funds for special learning instruction, for advanced placement courses. Increasingly parents face extra fees for programs. In Medina, Ohio, for example, it costs $660 to play a high school sport, $200 to join the school choir, $50 to act in a student play.

Even as budgets are slashed for public schools, more and more state education money is getting siphoned off to private contractors to pay for elaborate tests, and to vouchers and corporate tax credits to subsidize private and charter schools. We're cutting billions out of educating kids while increasing spending on testing how they are doing.

The Center for Budget and Policy Priorities reports that school budgets have been cut in some 34 states and the District of Columbia. In Arizona, the cuts average about $530 per pupil. In Florida, $1 billion was cut in next year's budget, or about $542 per student. Not surprisingly, these cuts fall hardest on the poorest districts that can't afford to make up for them the way more affluent districts can. The kids who have the greatest need for public education are suffering the deepest cuts.

Americans sensibly value education. Every political candidate promises our children will have the best education in the world. Yet Washington seems largely oblivious to the carnage taking place in our schools. Part of the president's American Jobs Act was special funding to avoid more teacher layoffs. A filibuster by Republican Senators kept that from even coming up for debate, much less a vote.

The Grim Reality of Spending Cuts

Meanwhile a furious argument continues about what standard teachers and schools should be held accountable to. The administration, still touting its Race to the Top program, wants the reauthorization of No Child Left Behind to set the standard that all children should be "college ready" by the year 2020. Senator [Tom] Harkin introduced a more sensible standard of requiring "continuous improvement" from all schools.

But schools are eliminating kindergarten, laying off teachers, cramming 35 kids in a class, cutting advanced placement classes, and levying steep fees for kids to be in the band or play on an athletic team. Continuous improvement? Race to the Top? The grim reality facing our kids mocks the rhetoric.

Jeff Bryant, author of the *Starving America's Public Schools* report, notes that there have been only two previous times since 1929 when this nation cut spending significantly on its children's education—once in the midst of the Great Depression and once in the midst of World War II. With schools facing budget cutbacks while the largest generation of kids since the boomers flood the classrooms, this is likely to be the third. The bankers who caused the mess got bailed out. The military budget exceeds Cold War levels. The richest 1% of Americans, who make as much as the bottom 60% of Americans, pay the lowest tax rates since the Great Depression. But our kids and their schools are getting the bill for an economic mess they didn't create. No wonder Occupy Wall Street [a protest movement] is spreading across the country.

> *"Merit-pay systems are . . . an essential tool for designing schools and systems that can excel in tight times."*

Merit Pay for Teachers Should Be Used to Improve Education

Frederick M. Hess

In the following viewpoint, Frederick M. Hess argues that paying teachers with a one-size-fits-all system is not the best method of compensation. Merit pay, he claims, can reward productivity and encourage the development of teaching talent in needed areas. He cautions against utilizing merit pay based on test scores alone and encourages a more dynamic system.

Frederick M. Hess is resident scholar and director of education policy studies at the American Enterprise Institute and author of The Same Thing Over and Over: How School Reformers Get Stuck in Yesterday's Ideas.

As you read, consider the following questions:

1. According to the author, what have step-and-lane pay scales in the teaching profession rewarded?

Frederick M. Hess, "Spend Money Like It Matters," *Educational Leadership*, vol. 68, no. 4, Dec–Jan 2010–2011, pp. 51–54. Permission conveyed through Copyright Clearance Center, Inc. Republished with permission of Educational Leadership.

2. Hess suggests that schools might pay an excellent reading teacher extra for what reason?

3. According to the author, what is the problem with merit pay based on past performance?

Do you think that employees who are good at their work ought to be rewarded, recognized, and have the chance to step up into new opportunities and responsibilities? I do. If you're with me on this, you embrace the principle of merit pay—whether you know it or not.

A Reasonable Assumption

Because, although we all have that childhood friend or distant cousin who lives on a commune somewhere and inveighs against the evils of bourgeois materialism, most of us think it makes sense for a talented, hardworking engineer, dentist, accountant, or babysitter to be rewarded for his or her efforts.

There are two crucial provisos here. First, endorsing this principle doesn't mean signing on to the raft of slack-jawed merit-pay proposals that would-be reformers have championed in recent years. Merit pay is only useful if it's done smart, which entails using it to help attract, retain, and make full use of talented educators.

Second, understand that there's no proof that rewarding talented, hardworking folks "works." You can comb through decades of economics journals and issues of the *Harvard Business Review* without finding any proof that paying and promoting good employees yields good results. The premise just seems like a reasonable assumption; you either buy it, or you don't.

That's how I come at merit pay. I don't imagine that paying bonuses for bumps in test scores, as though we were compensating traveling encyclopedia salesmen in the 1950s, is going to improve teaching or learning. And I don't think that value-added calculations are themselves a comprehensive or reliable measure of teacher quality, even in grades where we can calculate such numbers with a reasonable degree of statistical accuracy. But money and metrics are invaluable tools in shaping a 21st century teaching profession.

The Point of Merit Pay

The point of rethinking pay is not to bribe teachers into working harder. Rather, merit pay is a tool for redefining the contours of the profession. Today's step-and-lane pay scales, built around seniority and credits completed, suggest that the primary way to determine how much teachers are worth is how long they've been on the job and how many courses they've sat through. I don't believe that's a good or useful way to gauge a teacher's value.

There's nothing innately wrong with step-and-lane compensation. Indeed, when introduced in the first decades of the 20th century, it was a sensible response to the massive gender inequities that characterized schooling. At that time, women were routinely paid half as much as their male counterparts. Because male teachers were far more prevalent in the high schools, many districts employed de facto pay scales in which high school teachers dramatically outearned their K–8 counterparts for no discernible reason. In that era, standardizing pay made sense.

By the 1970s, however, schools could no longer depend on a captive influx of talent regardless of the terms of employment. Whereas limited alternatives had meant that more than half of women graduating from college became teachers in mid-20th-century America, the figure today is closer to 15 percent. Meanwhile, new college graduates are much less likely to stick to a job for long stretches, the competition for college-educated talent has intensified, and we can now more or less distinguish teachers who excel at helping students master important content and skills.

All this adds up to a new workforce environment in which the step-and-lane, industrial-era model that flourished as a best practice in post–World War II auto and steel plants is unduly confining. Step-and-lane pay is ill-suited to attracting and retaining talent in the new world of career changers, scarce talent, and heightened expectations.

Merit pay is not a substitute for high-quality instructional materials, pedagogy, or curriculum. Rather, rethinking pay can help make employees feel valued, make the teaching profession more attractive to potential entrants, and signal that professional norms are displacing those of the industrial model. None of this "fixes" schools, but it does establish a firmer, more quality-conscious basis for dramatic improvement.

The Issue of Productivity

As cash-strapped states and school systems look ahead to lean years, it's vital to recognize that one-size-fits-all pay is insensitive to questions of productivity. Although the term *productivity* is regarded as an irritant in most education conversations, it refers to nothing more than how much good a given employee can do. If one teacher is regarded by colleagues as a far more valued mentor than another, or if one reading instructor helps students master skills much more rapidly than another, it's axiomatic that some teachers do more good than others do (that is, that some are more productive than others).

One-size-fits-all compensation means that we're either paying the most effective employees too little, paying their less effective colleagues too much, or, most times, a little of each. In a world of scarce talent and limited resources, this is a problem. Savvy leaders recognize the benefits of steering resources to employees who do the most good, as these are the employees whom schools most need to keep and from whom they need to most effectively wring every ounce of skill.

Thus, a crucial element of a well-designed merit-pay system is rewarding employees who not only do a terrific job but also do so in a way that extends their effect on students and schools. Rewarding prized mentors who choose to mentor more colleagues (while continuing to get high marks from them) or boosting pay for terrific classroom teachers who choose to take on larger student loads (while continuing to excel) are ways to use limited resources to amplify the contributions of skilled professionals.

Using Pay to Solve Problems

One-size-fits-all pay also inhibits efforts to leverage the opportunities for differentiation and specialization that new technologies and staffing models offer, such as the use of part-time professionals by the Boston-based Citizen Schools. Today, school systems casually operate on the implicit assumption that most teachers will be similarly adept at everything. In a routine day, a 4th grade teacher who is a terrific English language arts instructor might teach reading for just 90 minutes. For schools blessed with such a teacher, this is an extravagant waste of talent, especially when one can stroll down the hallway and see a less adept colleague offering 90 minutes of pedestrian reading instruction. If we're sincere about the centrality of early reading proficiency, using these educators in this fashion is simply irresponsible.

One approach to using talent more wisely might entail overhauling teacher schedules and student assignment so that the single exceptional English language arts instructor would teach reading to every student in that 4th grade. Colleagues, in turn, would shoulder that teacher's other instructional responsibilities. However, this is not an even swap. Excellent reading instructors are rare; we should refashion compensation to recognize their importance. If that encourages other teachers to develop their skills and pursue this role, so much the better. Districts with a plethora of talent can then revise staffing accordingly. The point is that salary should be a tool for solving problems by finding smarter ways to attract, nurture, and use talent; it should not be an obstacle to doing so.

After all, we pay thoracic surgeons much more than we do pediatric nurses—not because we think they're better people or because they have lower patient mortality rates, but because their positions require more sophisticated skills and more intensive training and because surgeons are harder to replace. By allowing pay to reflect perceived value, law and medicine have made it possible for accomplished attorneys or doctors to earn outsized compensation without ever moving into administration or management. That kind of a model in education would permit truly revolutionary rethinking in how we recruit, retain, and deploy effective educators. That's a far cry from today's ill-conceived proposals to slather some test-based bonuses atop existing pay scales.

A Viable Path Forward

Unfortunately, too many would-be reformers hear the call for rethinking pay as a charge to impatiently rush forth and "fix" compensation in a furious burst of legislation. As a result, promising efforts to uproot outdated, stifling arrangements get enveloped in crudely drawn and potentially destructive policies.

Education reformers have trouble accepting that unwinding long-standing arrangements and replacing them with sensible alternatives will take time, humility, and a lot of learning. The fix-it-now approach to pay, with its overreliance on value-added measurements, turns a blind eye to the technical challenges involved and to the fact that reading and math scores are a profoundly limited proxy for instructional effectiveness. This approach also runs the risk of stifling the kind of smart use of personnel that reformers are trying to encourage. Principals who rotate their faculty by strength during the year or who augment classroom teachers with guest instructors or online lessons are going to clash with evaluation and pay systems predicated on linking each student's annual test scores to a single teacher. Even in the states that have spent the most time on these assessment and data systems, value-added scores are available for only a sliver of instruction and for only a minority of teachers. Devising new one-size-fits-all merit-pay systems around this limited population is both premature and nonsensical.

Right now, the smart move is to explore ways to base an increasing share of teacher pay on various measures of performance, drawing on potential metrics that seem useful and reliable in a given district. Labor market conditions should be a consideration; if it's more difficult to find effective math teachers than effective social studies teachers, pay should reflect that. In a world of accountability, there is an increased role for simple principal evaluation. Given the collaborative nature of much good teaching, it makes sense to import a key element of 360-degree evaluation and factor in systematic evaluations of teachers by their colleagues regarding which teachers make the largest contributions to the school and their peers. Measures of productivity; value-added calculations, where appropriate; and systematic classroom observation also have roles to play.

Just as many educators comfortable with step-and-lane pay recoil from such changes, many would-be reformers reject my counsel of patience and seek to "fix" teacher pay immediately. But K–12 is a sprawling, complex exercise. Spasmodic solutions born of frustration can lead to flawed policy—as with No Child Left Behind, which overreached in ways that undermined the law's more sensible provisions.

Designing the Right Merit-Pay Systems

Merit pay should reward performance, value, and productivity. We can measure these in many ways—by scarcity of individuals in the labor market, annual evaluation by peers, professional observations, supervisor judgment, and so forth. The contemporary obsession with student test scores as the only metric of interest has been an unfortunate distraction.

Student achievement must be an important factor, but we should employ it deliberately, with an eye to a teacher's actual instructional duties and responsibilities. Too often, we rely on test scores simply because we don't have anything else. That's not a problem specific to merit pay; that's our peculiar failure to import widely employed practices and tools from other professions.

Second, it's a mistake to imagine there's one universal way to design pay systems. Why debate about whether Google, the Red Cross, or Microsoft has the "right" compensation model? There are a slew of reasonable approaches, depending on organizational context and needs. Rather than searching for proven pay models, education leaders would be better off identifying the problems they're trying to address and asking how reconfiguring pay might help them solve those problems.

Third, the aim must be to craft systems that can evolve. The whole point of pay is to help attract and leverage talent. We need an approach that succeeds in tapping specialists, online instructors, part-time educators, and others who can best serve students. Rather than cement in place new merit-pay systems predicated on improving test scores for a teacher who spends 45 minutes a day for 180 days with the same 24 students, let's design systems that can reward unconventional forms of excellence.

For instance, an online tutor who lives thousands of miles away but who can help struggling students make remarkable leaps in mastery of algebra is an invaluable asset. The same is true of a retired army sergeant who may be ill-equipped to teach a middle school class but who may be able to inspire and mentor 15 middle school students or of a teacher who builds a dynamic arts or science program. Today, there is little room in teacher pay scales to recognize or reward—or, sometimes, even make possible—these kinds of contributions. The attempt to superimpose rigid hierarchies atop an otherwise unchanged profession was one of the big stumbling blocks for career ladders and merit-pay proposals in the 1980s. Let's take care not to repeat those mistakes.

Finally, today's test-based merit-pay systems have nothing to say when it comes to productivity. They funnel more dollars to teachers who yield higher test scores. The reward is a bonus for past performance; it does nothing to amplify a teacher's effect on students and schools. Well-designed merit-pay systems should reward teachers who choose to take up opportunities to do more good—such as instructing additional students, leveraging particular skills, or assisting colleagues—making their increased pay a pound-wise investment for their districts or schools.

This means that merit-pay systems are not, as some would argue, a frilly luxury that is unaffordable in today's bleak fiscal climate. Rather, they are an essential tool for designing schools and systems that can excel in tight times. Merit pay should shift dollars from employees and roles that do less good for students toward those that matter most. This will entail discomfort and disruption and require an array of compromises and adjustments. But if merit pay is to be more than a gimmick, it must be part and parcel of a push to rethink the shape of teaching and schooling.

| "Merit pay [based on test scores] will not make education better."

What's Wrong with Merit Pay?

Diane Ravitch

In the following viewpoint, Diane Ravitch argues that merit pay based on test scores is misguided and will make education worse. Ravitch contends that merit pay used in this way rewards results in a very narrow portion of the curriculum. Regardless, she claims that research shows merit pay has no impact on test scores.

Diane Ravitch is a research professor of education at New York University, a senior fellow at the Brookings Institution, and former assistant secretary of education responsible for the Office of Educational Research and Improvement in the US Department of Education.

As you read, consider the following questions:

1. According to the author, merit pay for increased test scores encourages teachers to teach only what?

2. A merit-pay experiment in New York City cost taxpayers how much annually, according to Ravitch?

3. Which subjects does Ravitch claim will get too little attention in school if merit pay based on test scores is utilized?

The subject today is merit pay, an important topic because President Obama has decided to hang his hat on this idea. It has not yet been explained, however, just what he means by merit pay. Does he mean that teachers should be paid more for teaching in what are euphemistically called "hard to staff" schools? Paid more for teaching in areas where there are shortages, such as certain kinds of special education or subjects such as math and science? Or paid more for mentoring other teachers or teaching longer days?

I would call such compensation "performance pay," rather than merit pay, because teachers would be paid more for doing more. But I have a feeling that what the Obama administration has in mind is paying teachers more based on their students' "value-added" test scores, meaning that when their students' scores increase, the teachers will get "merit pay" to reward their supposedly superior teaching.

I believe that this is the direction in which the administration is heading, which explains why millions of dollars will be spent on data warehouses in every state and why Education Secretary Arne Duncan has told the governors that they will get their stimulus money only if they collect and report data to the federal government. This was an odd request in that some of the information he asked for is already available, such as the gap between state and National Assessment of Educational Progress scores (data previously published and no secret).

There are several reasons why it is a bad idea to pay teachers extra for raising student test scores. Doing so would

- Create incentives for teachers to teach only what is on the tests of reading and math, thus narrowing the curriculum to only the subjects tested;

- Encourage not only teaching to the test but gaming the system by such mechanisms as excluding low-performing students and outright cheating;

- Ignore a wealth of studies showing that student test scores are subject to statistical errors, measurement errors, and random errors and that the "noise" in these scores is multiplied when used to make high-stakes personnel decisions;

- Overlook the fact that most teachers in a school are not eligible for such "merit" bonuses—only those who teach reading and math and only those for whom scores can be obtained in a previous year;

- Fail to acknowledge that many factors play a role in student test scores, including student ability, student motivation, family support (or lack thereof), the weather, distractions on testing day, and so on;

- Not reckon with the fact that tests must be given at the beginning and the end of the year, not midyear as is now the practice in many states. (Which teacher would get credit and a bonus for score gains: the one who taught the student in the spring of the previous year or the one who taught her in the fall?)

I believe that merit pay of the stupidest kind is coming and that it will do nothing to improve our schools. The Manhattan Institute recently released a study showing that merit pay had no impact on test scores in 200 New York City schools that had tried it. In fact, scores went down in larger schools that offered bonuses. (It is possible that scores may go up in later years; this is only the first year, after all.) But this little experiment in schoolwide bonuses is costing taxpayers $20 million a year.

The way in which this study was released is highly interesting. Usually when the Manhattan Institute releases a study,

A Study of Merit Pay

In this paper we present evidence on the impact of NYCDOE's SPBP [New York City Department of Education's School-Wide Performance Bonus Program] during the program's first year of implementation. Because the number of schools meeting eligibility criteria under the SPBP guidelines required more than the amount of money budgeted for the program, NYCDOE's Research and Policy Support Group assigned schools to the SPBP intervention by random lottery. Our evaluation design takes advantage of the fact that schools were randomly lotteried into the SPBP intervention.

Our findings suggest that the SPBP has had negligible short-run effects on student achievement in mathematics. The same holds true for intermediate outcomes such as student, parent, and teacher perceptions of the school learning environment. We also find no evidence that the treatment effect differed on the basis of student or school characteristic. An exception is the differential effect of SPBP eligibility by school size, which suggests student performance in larger schools decreases when SPBP was implemented. . . .

Although a well-implemented experimental evaluation design would suggest that our estimates have strong internal validity, readers should interpret these initial findings with caution when considering the possible impact of this or any other program.

Matthew G. Springer and Marcus A. Winters, Center for Civic Innovation at the Manhattan Institute, April 2009.

it holds a press conference to announce the results. This study, however, arrived with no fanfare; its results were quietly posted on the web with no press conference, no press release. I suspect that had the scores flown upward, the study would have been released with all the bells and whistles.

My prediction is that merit pay of the kind I have described will not make education better, even if scores go up next year or the year after. Instead, it will make education worse, not only because some of the purported gains will be based on cheating and gaming the system but because they will have been obtained by paying scant attention to history, geography, civics, the arts, science, literature, foreign languages, and all the other subjects needed to develop smarter individuals, better citizens, and people who are prepared for the knowledge-based economy of the twenty-first century. Nor will it identify better teachers. Instead, it will reward those who use their time for low-level test preparation.

Is it possible to have an educational system that miseducates students while raising their test scores? I think so—and we may soon prove it.

Periodical and Internet Sources Bibliography

The following articles have been selected to supplement the diverse views presented in this chapter.

Andrew Biggs and Jason Richwine	"Public School Teachers Aren't Underpaid," *USA Today*, November 16, 2011.
Bruce Buchanan	"Beyond the Basics," *American School Board Journal*, May 2008.
Dana Goldstein	"Is Merit Pay a Distraction in the Fight for Meaningful Education Reform?," *American Prospect*, March 30, 2009.
Susan Harman	"Pay-per-Score: Arne Duncan and Merit Pay," *Dissent*, July 9, 2009.
Frederick M. Hess and Linda Darling-Hammond	"How to Rescue Education Reform," *New York Times*, December 5, 2011.
Jim Hull	"Cutting to the Bone: At a Glance," Center for Public Education, October 2010. www.centerforpubliceducation.org/Main-Menu/ Public-education/Cutting-to-the-bone-At-a-glance.
Neal McCluskey	"Behind the Curtain: Assessing the Case for National Curriculum Standards," *Cato Policy Analysis*, February 17, 2010.
John Merrow	"The Influence of Teachers," *Independent School*, Winter 2008.
Kenneth A. Strike	"Small Schools: Size or Community?," *American Journal of Education*, May 2008.
Joel Westheimer	"No Child Left Thinking," *Independent School*, Spring 2008.

For Further Discussion

Chapter 1

1. Amanda Ripley and Gerald W. Bracey disagree about what the comparative performance of American students says about the US education system. Do the two disagree about the facts of the research, the interpretation of the research, or both? Explain your answer, citing from the viewpoints.

2. Terry M. Moe and Richard D. Kahlenberg have competing views about the impact of the teachers' unions on education. How do you think Kahlenberg would respond to Moe's concern about the difficulties schools face in getting rid of bad teachers?

Chapter 2

1. Andrew Bernstein believes that the privatization of government-run public schools will lead to more freedom for parents in educational choices, whereas Ruth Conniff raises concerns that privatization will remove educational control from communities. Based on what each of them argues, do you think privatization would lead to more educational freedom or less? Explain your answer, citing from the viewpoints.

2. Both Matthew McKnight and the National Education Association argue against alternatives to public school—through vouchers and tax credits, respectively—due to how the programs will affect the most disadvantaged students in the current system. What solution might a proponent of school-choice alternatives, such as Gary Jason or David French, offer in an attempt to alleviate this concern?

Chapter 3

1. Among the viewpoints of John W. Whitehead, Americans United for Separation of Church and State, and Kurt Williamsen, which two viewpoints are the most compatible? Explain your answer.

2. Satoshi Kanazawa uses an analogy between the refusal to teach creationism and intelligent design in schools and the refusal to teach about capitalism in former communist countries. List the ways in which the two are not analogous and then assess whether this is a strong analogy for Kanazawa's purpose.

3. What is the core disagreement between Casey Luskin and Heather Weaver on the issue of teaching debate about evolution in public schools? Why?

Chapter 4

1. Frederick M. Hess argues in favor of developing effective merit-pay systems. Based on the content of his viewpoint calling for cuts in education spending, do you think Neal McCluskey could endorse Hess's proposal? Why or why not?

2. Diane Ravitch argues against a particular kind of merit pay. Do you think she would endorse the kind of merit-pay systems proposed by Frederick M. Hess? Explain your answer.

Organizations to Contact

The editors have compiled the following list of organizations concerned with the issues debated in this book. The descriptions are derived from materials provided by the organizations. All have publications or information available for interested readers. The list was compiled on the date of publication of the present volume; the information provided here may change. Be aware that many organizations take several weeks or longer to respond to inquiries, so allow as much time as possible.

American Civil Liberties Union (ACLU)
125 Broad Street, 18th Floor, New York, NY   10004
(212) 549-2500
e-mail: infoaclu@aclu.org
website: www.aclu.org

The American Civil Liberties Union is a national organization that works to defend Americans' civil rights as guaranteed in the US Constitution. The ACLU works in courts, legislatures, and communities to defend First Amendment rights to freedom of speech, freedom of the press, and freedom of religion; the right to equal protection; the right to due process; and the right to privacy. The ACLU publishes the semiannual newsletter *Civil Liberties Alert*, as well as other publications, including "ACLU History: Maintaining the Wall: Freedom of—and from—Religion."

American Policy Center (APC)
PO Box 129, Remington, VA   22734
(540) 341-8911
e-mail: admin@americanpolicy.org
website: www.americanpolicy.org

The American Policy Center is a privately funded, nonprofit, grassroots action and educational foundation dedicated to the promotion of free enterprise and limited government regulations of commerce and individuals. The APC focuses on the issues of environmental policy and its effect on private property rights; national federal computer data banks and their effect on individual privacy rights; the United Nations and its effect on American national sovereignty; and federal education policy and its effect on local schools and parental rights. APC publishes *The DeWeese Report* and special reports on the above issues.

Americans United for Separation of Church and State (AU)
1301 K Street NW, Suite 850E, Washington, DC   20005
(202) 466-3234 • fax: (202) 466-2587
e-mail: americansunited@au.org
website: www.au.org

Americans United for Separation of Church and State is a nonprofit educational organization dedicated to preserving the constitutional principle of church-state separation. AU works to defend religious liberty in Congress and state legislatures, aiming to ensure that new legislation and policies protect church-state separation. AU publishes several books and pamphlets, including *Religion in the Public Schools: A Road Map for Avoiding Lawsuits and Respecting Parents' Legal Rights*.

Becket Fund for Religious Liberty
3000 K Street NW, Suite 220, Washington, DC   20007
(202) 955-0095 • fax: (202) 955-0090
website: www.becketfund.org

The Becket Fund for Religious Liberty is a public-interest law firm protecting the free expression of all religious traditions. Among other practice areas, the Becket Fund defends private religious expression by public school students and works to ensure that private religious schools can educate students without government interference or discrimination. At its website, the Becket Fund has information about its legal cases, including its US Supreme Court case briefs.

Cato Institute
1000 Massachusetts Ave. NW, Washington, DC   20001-5403
(202) 842-0200 • fax: (202) 842-3490
website: www.cato.org

The Cato Institute is a public-policy research organization dedicated to the principles of individual liberty, limited government, free markets, and peace. The institute is dedicated to increasing and enhancing the understanding of key public policies and to analyzing their impact on the principles identified above in many research areas, including education and child policy. The Cato Institute issues many publications, including the quarterly *Regulation* magazine, the bimonthly *Cato Policy Report*, and the periodic *Cato Journal*.

Center for Education Reform (CER)
910 Seventeenth Street NW, 11th Floor
Washington, DC   20006
(800) 521-2118
website: www.edreform.org

The Center for Education Reform aims to improve the accuracy and quality of discourse and decisions about education reform, leading to fundamental policy changes. The CER campaigns for policies that create more educational choice, including the establishment of charter schools. The CER website offers numerous articles on issues such as charter schools, online learning, teacher quality, and standards and testing.

Center for Public Education
1680 Duke Street, Alexandria, VA   22314
(703) 838-6722 • fax: (703) 548-5613
e-mail: centerforpubliced@nsba.org
website: www.centerforpubliceducation.org

The Center for Public Education is a resource center set up by the National School Boards Association. The center works to provide information about public education, leading to more understanding about US schools, more community-wide involvement, and better decision making by school leaders on behalf of all students in their classrooms. Among the many publications available at the center's website is "The Changing Demographics of America's Schools."

Center for Science & Culture (CSC)

Discovery Institute, Seattle, WA   98104
(206) 292-0401 • fax: (206) 682-5320
e-mail: cscinfo@discovery.org
website: www.discovery.org/csc

The Center for Science & Culture is a Discovery Institute program that supports research by scientists and other scholars challenging various aspects of neo-Darwinian evolution theory and developing the theory of intelligent design. The CSC also encourages schools to focus more on weaknesses of the theory of evolution in science education. The CSC has numerous papers, policy positions and videos available on its website, including *Teaching About Evolution in the Public Schools: A Short Summary of the Law.*

Center on Education Policy (CEP)

2140 Pennsylvania Ave. NW, Room 103, Washington, DC 20037
(202) 994-9050 • fax: (202) 994-8859
e-mail: cep-dc@cep-dc.org
website: www.cep-dc.org

The Center on Education Policy is a national, independent advocate for public education and for more effective public schools. The organization works on national, state, and local levels to inform the government and the public, via publications, meetings, and presentations, about the importance of the public education system. Reports on issues regarding all aspects of the education system, such as federal education programs, testing, vouchers, and ways to improve public schools, can be found on the CEP website.

Character Education Partnership
1025 Connecticut Ave. NW, Suite 1011
Washington, DC   20036
(202) 296-7743
website: www.character.org

The Character Education Partnership is a nonprofit, nonpartisan, nonsectarian coalition of organizations and individuals committed to fostering effective character education in schools. It provides tools, methods, and strategies to empower teachers, parents, and community members to help schools achieve the goals of character development. The partnership publishes annual reports assessing the status of character education in the United States, and also provides online resources such as "11 Principles of Effective Character Education."

Education Commission of the States (ECS)
700 Broadway, #810, Denver, CO   80203-3442
(303) 299-3600 • fax: (303) 296-8332
e-mail: ecs@ecs.org
website: www.ecs.org

The Education Commission of the States is an interstate compact created in 1965 to improve public education by facilitating the exchange of information, ideas, and experiences among state policy makers and education leaders. As a nonprofit, nonpartisan organization involving key leaders from all levels of the education system, ECS creates unique opportunities to build partnerships, share information, and promote the development of policy based on available research and strategies. ECS provides policy research and analysis on current educational issues; sponsors state, regional, and national policy conferences; and publishes the bimonthly journal the *Progress of Education Reform*.

First Amendment Center
1207 Eighteenth Ave. South, Nashville, TN   37212
(615) 727-1600 • fax: (615) 727-1319
website: www.firstamendmentcenter.org

The First Amendment Center works to preserve and protect First Amendment freedoms by providing information and education. The center serves as a forum for the study and exploration of free-expression issues, including freedom of speech, of the press, and of religion, and the rights to assemble and to petition the government. The First Amendment Center publishes a number of articles, including "Evolution and Creation."

Friedman Foundation for Educational Choice

One American Square, Suite 2420, Indianapolis, IN 46282
(317) 681-0745 • fax: (317) 681-0945
website: www.edchoice.org

The Friedman Foundation aims to promote universal school choice as the most effective and equitable way to improve the quality of K–12 education in America. The foundation was founded upon the ideals and theories of Nobel laureate economist Milton Friedman and economist Rose D. Friedman, who believed that when schools are forced to compete to keep the children they educate, all parties win. The Friedman Foundation publishes studies and reports such as "Moms and Schools Survey," available at its website.

National Center for Fair & Open Testing (FairTest)

PO Box 300204, Jamaica Plain, MA 02130
(617) 477-9792
website: www.fairtest.org

The National Center for Fair & Open Testing advances quality education and equal opportunity by promoting fair, open, valid, and educationally beneficial evaluations of students, teachers, and schools. FairTest's Assessment Reform Network aims to facilitate the exchange of information and ideas among teachers, parents, and organizations seeking to improve student assessment practices in their communities. FairTest publishes numerous fact sheets available at its website, including "A Better Way to Evaluate Schools."

National Education Association (NEA)
1201 Sixteenth Street NW, Washington, DC   20036-3290
(202) 833-4000 • fax: (202) 822-7974
website: www.nea.org

The National Education Association is an educator membership organization that works to advance the cause of public
education and the rights of educators and children. The NEA
focuses its efforts on improving the quality of teaching, increasing student achievement, and making schools safe places
to learn. Among the magazines that the NEA publishes are
NEA Today and *Thought & Action*.

Progressive Policy Institute (PPI)
1101 Fourteenth Street NW, Suite 1250
Washington, DC   20005
(202) 525-3926 • fax: (202) 525-3941
website: www.progressivepolicy.org

The Progressive Policy Institute works to advance progressive,
market-friendly ideas that promote American innovation, economic growth, and wider opportunity. Numerous articles can
be found on the PPI website, including such titles as "Improving Charter School Accountability: The Challenge of Closing
Failing Schools."

US Department of Education
400 Maryland Ave. SW, Washington, DC   20202
(800) 872-5327
website: www.ed.gov

The US Department of Education's mission is to promote student achievement and preparation for global competitiveness
by fostering educational excellence and ensuring equal access.
It engages in the following four major types of activity: 1) establishing policies related to federal education funding, ad-
ministering distribution of funds and monitoring their use; 2)
collecting data and overseeing research on America's schools;
3) identifying major issues in education and focusing national

attention on them; 4) enforcing federal laws prohibiting dis-crimination in programs that receive federal funds. The De-partment of Education publishes a variety of newsletters on specific topics relating to education, and its National Center for Education Statistics compiles annual information through its National Assessment of Educational Progress (NAEP).

Bibliography of Books

Phil Boyle and
Del Burns

Preserving the Public *in Public Schools: Visions, Values, Conflicts, and Choices.* Lanham, MD: Rowman and Littlefield Education, 2012.

Dave F. Brown

Why America's Public Schools Are the Best Place for Kids: Reality vs. Negative Perceptions. Lanham, MD: Rowman and Littlefield Education, 2011.

Evans Clinchy

Rescuing the Public Schools: What It Will Take to Leave No Child Behind. New York: Teachers College Press, 2007.

Lisa D. Delpit

Multiplication Is for White People: Raising Expectations for Other People's Children. New York: New Press, 2012.

Sara Dimerman

Character Is the Key: How to Unlock the Best in Our Children and Ourselves. Hoboken, NJ: Wiley, 2009.

Julie Duckworth

The Little Book of Values: Educating Children to Become Thinking, Responsible, and Caring Citizens. Bethel, CT: Crown House, 2009.

Greg Forster and
C. Bradley
Thompson, eds.

Freedom and School Choice in American Education. New York: Palgrave Macmillan, 2011.

Charles L. Glenn — *Contrasting Models of State and School: A Comparative Historical Study of Parental Choice and State Control.* New York: Continuum, 2011.

Steven K. Green — *The Bible, the School, and the Constitution: The Clash That Shaped Modern Church-State Doctrine.* New York: Oxford University Press, 2012.

Jay P. Greene — *Why America Needs School Choice.* New York: Continuum, 2011.

H. Wayne House, ed. — *Intelligent Design 101: Leading Experts Explain the Key Issues.* Grand Rapids, MI: Kregel, 2008.

William H. Jeynes — *A Call for Character Education and Prayer in the Schools.* Santa Barbara, CA: Praeger, 2010.

Emile Lester — *Teaching About Religions: A Democratic Approach for Public Schools.* Ann Arbor: University of Michigan Press, 2011.

Judd Kruger Levingston — *Sowing the Seeds of Character: The Moral Education of Adolescents in Public and Private Schools.* Westport, CT: Praeger, 2009.

Charles Murray — *Real Education: Four Simple Truths for Bringing America's Schools Back to Reality.* New York: Random House, 2009.

Warren A. Nord — *Does God Make a Difference? Taking Religion Seriously in Our Schools and Universities.* New York: Oxford University Press, 2010.

Diane Ravitch — *The Death and Life of the Great American School System: How Testing and Choice Are Undermining Education.* New York: Basic Books, 2010.

Mike Rose — *Why School? Reclaiming Education for All of Us.* New York: New Press, 2009.

H. Svi Shapiro, ed. — *Education and Hope in Troubled Times: Visions of Change for Our Children's World.* New York: Routledge, 2009.

Stephen D. Solomon — *Ellery's Protest: How One Young Man Defied Tradition and Sparked the Battle over School Prayer.* Ann Arbor: University of Michigan Press, 2009.

Joel Spring — *American Education*, 15th ed. New York: McGraw-Hill, 2012.

Keith Stewart Thomson — *Before Darwin: Reconciling God and Nature.* New Haven, CT: Yale University Press, 2008.

Paul Tough — *How Children Succeed: Grit, Curiosity, and the Hidden Power of Character.* Boston: Houghton Mifflin Harcourt, 2012.

Herbert J. Walberg — *Tests, Testing, and Genuine School Reform.* Stanford, CA: Education Next Books, 2011.

Bob Wise   *Raising the Grade: How High School
                Reform Can Save Our Youth and Our
                Nation.* San Francisco: Jossey-Bass,
                2008.

Index